NEAR THE TORII GATE

A Zen Journey in Photographs and Poetry

NEAR THE TORII GATE
A Zen Journey in Photographs and Poetry

FIRST EDITION
© 2010

PUBLISHED BY
DON ALBRECHT PHOTOGRAPHY
Bayfield, Wisconsin

Albrecht, Don 1949-
Saetre, David 1951-

ISBN 978-1-4507-1069-5

Book design and photography by Don Albrecht
Poetry by David Saetre
Foreword and translations by Dr. Leslie Alldritt, with Junko Ladd
Edited by Mary M. V. Hunter

Connecting to the "Subtle Profundity" of Japan
by Leslie D. Alldritt

Japan is a wondrous place. When I travel there now, I feel a sense of what I can only describe as relief, a homecoming. As I work my way through customs and come through the door into the general airport, see the familiar signs, hear the rhythms of Japanese spoken around me and over the airport intercom, my body and mind settle into a comfortable place that only being in Japan provides.

In May 1878, Isabella Bird, an intrepid, Victorian woman, landed in Yokohama, Japan. Ostensibly there for her health, she was really there to sate her curiosity. During her seven-month stay, she produced an unusually frank, if not always well-informed or non-prejudicial, account of the sights of the Meiji Period Japan she encountered.

In May 2007, five faculty colleagues and I also landed in Japan. Four of us set foot on Japan for the first time, as with Bird; two of us were return visitors. We traveled in a different part of Japan at a very different time, yet I find it intriguing to compare our experiences with those of Isabella Bird.

Bird's challenges with accommodations included constant warfare with fleas and other insects and unclean rooms in *yadoyas* (inns). Her varied conveyances en route included *jinrikisha*, horse, train, and even a cow at one point, aided by runners and coolies to support her. Our party did reside at Japanese inns (*ryokan, minshuku*) and temples but found them comfortable and agreeable to the Japan we sought to explore. Traveling by train, subways, ferry, cable car, and bus allowed us to jostle beside the average Japanese citizen, and other foreigners, now as equals rather than subordinates.

Food, of course, is an important part of any international trip. Bird's trip was no exception; she packed a "small supply of Liebig's extract of meat, 4 lbs. of raisins, some chocolate, and some brandy" as she set out for the interior. Her view of Japanese cuisine differed sharply from our experience. She reported "fresh fish is rare," and "the fishy and vegetable abominations known as 'Japanese food' can only be swallowed and digested by a few, and that after long practice." Our group experienced the wonder of Japanese cuisine, including *okonomiyaki* in Hiroshima, *kaiten-zushi* (conveyor-belt sushi) in Kyoto, and, memorably, the exquisite temple dishes (*shōjin ryōri*) of Koyasan as we joined other pilgrims in a *shukubō*

(temple stay).

Bird really does, after all her hardships, admire Japan. Her detailed account of visiting Asakusa temple in Yedo (*Tokio*) is wonderfully evocative and is quite similar to our frequent stops at noted Buddhist temples. She remarks that although traveling as a foreign woman alone at a time and location in which this was exceedingly rare, she did not meet with "a single instance of incivility or real overcharge" and adds "there is no rudeness even about the crowding." Japanese do most often uphold the virtue of civility and politeness, although sometimes the crowds do test them! In all my travels to Japan over the years, the genial attitude and kindness of the Japanese people hold most constant.

Bird even comes to grasp the singularity of Japanese aesthetics. She reports, "I am beginning to appreciate the extreme beauty of solitude in decoration. In the alcove hangs a *kakemono* (scroll) of exquisite beauty, a single blossoming branch of the cherry.

What would Isabella Bird have thought of the book now in your hands? I believe she would have noted that the images and poetry within abundantly reflected what she sought in coming to Japan, and what our traveling party, too, was seeking—the heart (*kokoro*) of Japan. She states the "real Japan" is what she wants to experience; I hope she came to realize the "real Japan" is simply Japan *as it is*. I find this book to ring out this view: here is Japan just *as it is*.

An attempt to capture the wonder of Japan through any artistic form, is, of course, failed from conception. Over the centuries, artistic masters of different abilities have made countless efforts. However, to my mind, the most successful attempts have been by those artists who connected with the "subtle profundity" that abides in Japanese religion and art. As I study Don's photos and David's poetry, I believe this collection joins those successful attempts.

I would be quite remiss to conclude this foreword without a few words of gratitude. Our faculty development trip to Japan would not have been possible save for the support of Northland College and in particular, the Provost, Rick Fairbanks, and the Advancement Office. One could not have asked for a better traveling party, so heartfelt thanks are due to my faculty colleagues: Michele Small, Jason Terry, Tim Doyle and, of course, Don and David.

Many flowers bloomed from this trip. I am so happy that Don and David have gathered these visual and verbal flowers and now choose to share their evocative aroma and beauty with us.

Leslie Alldritt savors a quiet moment to himself at Tekishinjuku, the International Zen Center near Kameoka. Dr. Alldritt is former Distinguished Hulings Chair in the Humanities and current Professor of Religion at Northland College.

ABOUT THE FACULTY SEMINAR

The Way of Tea and Other Exquisite Experiences

In 2007, six professors from Ashland, Wisconsin spent three life-changing weeks living, traveling and studying in Japan, the "land of the rising sun." We were privileged to share this experience—the inaugural international faculty development seminar offered by and for Northland College faculty members—with four colleagues: Professors Tim Doyle (Philosophy), Jason Terry (Art), Michele Small (English), and Leslie Alldritt (Religion).

Professor Alldritt conceived the idea for such an interdisciplinary seminar during a student study trip he previously led to Japan. Alldritt has had a long association with Japan. As a graduate student, he lived in Kyoto for two academic years and, during his 19 years at Northland College, he has traveled frequently to Japan for research.

While staying at Matsubaya Ryokan, we walked and took the bus or train to many of Kyoto's Buddhist temples, Shinto shrines, Zen gardens and teahouses, and had easy high-speed train access to other sites on Japan's main island of Honshu. The *Shinkansen* (bullet train) took us to visit Northland College's Japanese sister college, Hagoromo Kokusai Daigaku, in Osaka. We wove our way back and forth between ancient Japan and modern Japan, as do many Japanese citizens in their daily lives.

We spent three days in full immersion study of Zen Buddhism at Tekishinjuku, the International Zen Center in Kameoka, simultaneously encountering Buddhism and encountering ourselves. Additional day trips allowed us to visit a mountaintop region called Kurama, the peace park and museum at Hiroshima, and the extraordinary sacred mountain Koyasan with its huge cemetery and many Buddhist temples. In the old imperial city of Nara, we considered Buddhist art treasures and temples 1300 years old. Miyajima, site of Japan's most famous shrine, was a short journey from Hiroshima by cable car and ferry.

All six of us had intense and exquisite experiences, as reflected in subsequent scholarly writings, art exhibitions, on-campus and community presentations, and in ongoing reflection and creative output. The poetry and photography we present in this book comprise one small set of creative outcomes from this inspiring journey to the place of the sun's origin.

Tea master Bruce Hemana from the Urasenke Tea Center in Kyoto presented the Japanese Way of Tea, emphasizing harmony, respect, tranquility and purity, to the Northland College International Faculty Seminar (left to right) Michele Small, Don Albrecht, Bruce Hemana, Leslie Alldritt, Jason Terry, David Saetre, and Tim Doyle.

Photographs Are Living Things

by Don Albrecht

Photographs, like many of the fine arts, are a tangible embodiment of time and meaning. Whenever you look at a photograph with a discerning eye, you don't just see—you sense with the full depth of human capacity. The images move. They ring with sound. They leap off the page. They enter in. They are alive.

As an artist, I have put increasing emphasis on the book form as a self-contained and intimate method for sharing my work. I still exhibit work in galleries, but I find that books allow me to sequence and size work to a format that you can hold in your hands and contemplate over time.

This form also allows complementing images with words—in this case, magical poetry from a close friend who shared the experience. I find it fitting that David's poems are written in the present tense. I take my cue from one of my photography mentors, Arno Rafael Minkkinen, who wrote that "when writing about photographs, it's natural to write in the present tense. That's because photographs are living things."

When I look at my photographs from the 2007 trip, I see an enormous difference between my black & white film work and my color digital photography. I have to shift my mind depending on which camera I choose for a specific exposure. The digital camera coughs up good documentary evidence of what I see, despite any judgment, in full living color—accurate, precise, undistorted. Digital photographs, in all their colorful glory, are my "window" to the world.

Don Albrecht set down his cameras long enough to swing the striker pole of an ancient Buddhist bell at Miyajima's Daishoin Temple.

I made the black & white photographs you see in this book using a Holga camera—an all-plastic, anti-technical device I use because it unleashes artistic intuition. The Holga is my "mirror." Its foibles align to my own inner idiosyncrasies. Sometimes I don't see clearly: The world wiggles and shimmies, a jumble of confused lines and shapes. When I cannot understand what I'm seeing, the Holga helps me capture my inner uncertainty with more outward honesty than I may wish to admit.

The Holga camera uses 120 film, producing a nice, medium-sized negative that I then scan into a computer. Those digital files then went directly into the production of this book. No manipulation, no doctoring. Just photographs in the moment.

May you enjoy your own encounters with these "moments" David and I offer you, our entwined glimpses of the fascinating and profound culture of Japan.

ABOUT THE POETRY

Haiku and Zen: Language and This Moment

by David Saetre

I first became interested in haiku poetry as an undergraduate student in the late 1960s and early '70s. Like many other youth of that era, I first encountered the poetry through the wave of interest in Zen Buddhism that rolled across the Pacific and the California coast to campuses throughout the United States. The Beat writers—Ginsberg, Kerouac and, later, Snyder—introduced Zen and Zen arts to an alienated generation that longed for an alternative to the dominant Western culture.

Writing some years later, Zen teacher Masao Abe characterized the mood well: "Today, many people feel alienated and rootless. They have lost their home, their place of ultimate rest. The prevailing way of thinking has severed our age-old connection with our spiritual home." One could argue that the same conditions persist today. Japanese arts and religion promise a means to reconnect with life at its most basic, experiential level.

Haiku poetry, like Zen Buddhism, requires full awareness of the present moment, no more and no less. The poet observes, connects and reports the moment. T. H. Barrett said, "The art of haiku is to frame reality in single instant that will lock the poet and the reader into sharing the same experience." The poet gives voice to those moments that cannot be captured by discursive reason yet whose evocative power moves one at the deepest levels of experience.

Haiku, so lean and spare, so focused and simple, has a moving and elusive quality to it. This comes, in part, from the aesthetic values underlying Japanese Buddhism. One senses the spare simplicity characterized by the term *wabi*, and the melancholy produced by the passage of time, captured by the idea of *sabi*. A careful reader may also be moved by the prevailing awareness of the ephemeral beauty of the world where change is the only constant. The Japanese keenly described this "pity of all things" as *mono no aware*. Finally, the poetic form of haiku alludes to the inexpressible and ineffable quality of peak experience. The term *yugen* describes this awareness of the transcendent captured in the immanent moment—a longing anticipation of that which lies just beyond the horizon of our perception.

The art of haiku seeks to express those aesthetic values—simplicity, the patina of time, the melancholy of beauty and the awareness of something beyond—all captured in a moment. Not just any moment, but *this moment*—the moment experienced and rendered by the poet. Haiku communicates that experience and is not a commentary about it. Understanding that intent is a key to reading haiku. Each word of the haiku, then, is an experience as well. And sometimes, for the poet and the reader, an "a-ha!" happens. A moment of recognition—recognition of the world, the self and each other—evoking a shared smile or the solidarity of sorrow. All of this contained within three lines consisting of 17 syllables! What challenging and deceiving simplicity.

Haiku may be the most widely recognizable poetic form in the world. It evolved from classical Japanese poetry, called *waka*. Waka typically employed three opening phrases consisting of 5, 7 and 5 syllables, followed by additional verses. Japanese medieval court poetry favored a form called *tanka*, consisting of 31 syllables: 5-7-5-7-7. The first three lines of the various longer poetic forms became known as *hokku*. The 17th century bard, Matsuo Bashō, liberated those first lines from the boundaries of longer forms, creating what we know today as haiku.

Haiku in English poses certain problems when compared to the classical Japanese form. English syllables poorly approximate Japanese characters, and traditional Japanese haiku are usually rendered in a single line. I have tried to honor the meter of the classical form and I've chosen to follow the English standard of three separate lines. Japanese haiku employ specific words that create a sudden break and a sense of surprise or revelation. I've attempted to use punctuation to create the same effect. Most of my poems employ a traditional seasonal reference characteristic of an acute awareness of time and place. However, like the poems of many Japanese masters, my poems are not bound to a strict schema. They rather seek to capture the fullness of poetic awareness in a few words.

I wrote these poems during our 2007 travel seminar. As such, the poems share a noble tradition called *haibun*, mastered by Bashō, in which the writer uses poetry to evoke the intimate experience of his or her journey. The poetic

David Saetre contemplates the garden outside the Buddhist temple on Koyasan, where our group spent two nights.

rendering of my travel observations seemed to fit perfectly with the toy camera black-and-white images of my friend, photographer Don Albrecht. The immediacy, simplicity and evocative character of his photos make them wonderful companions to the art of haiku.

    Don and I did discuss the idea of creating this book while we were in Japan, but our poems and photographs originated independently of each other. I edited a few of the poems later, either to better reflect the original poetic experience or to make sense in relationship to the companion photograph.

    In these verbal and visual images I hope we communicate our sense of awareness and a way of being present in the world where even the simplest moment resonates, vibrates and pulses with wonder. And, perhaps, on a page here or there, you too will sense a spiritual connection to the world as our age-old home.

NEAR THE TORII GATE

Near the *torii* gate,

the wedding ends, as the tides

go in and out again.

鳥居門

結婚式終え

客の出入り

If you want to see
the Buddha you must sit down,
still, upon the ground.

御仏に
お会いしたいなら
黙って正座

Sound of an old pond

Sound of a mountain graveyard

Sound of an old monk.

古池の音

山の墓所の音

老僧の音

Koyasan

The moon alone lights
the path through Okunoin.
Two friends find their way
without a word between them,
walking among ancient graves.

高野山

奥の院
参道照らす
月明かり
友ふたり
静かに歩く
古墓を

Curl of smoke rising

from the zazen incense stick:

rising mountain mists.

座禅線香の

煙がうねる

山の霧

A gateless walk

the moon has risen by day, still

the taste of warm tea.

門のない

朝の月あり

温かい

茶の味わい

A modern tombstone
like a work of science fiction,
strangely out of place
rising out of ancient graves,
standing over the dead.

モダンな墓
SFのよう
場に合わず
古墓で
死体の上に
そびえ立つ

Here where two feet stand
two feet stand. Whose feet are these?
Mine, yours, Siddhartha's?

僕と君
ここに立つのは
仏もか

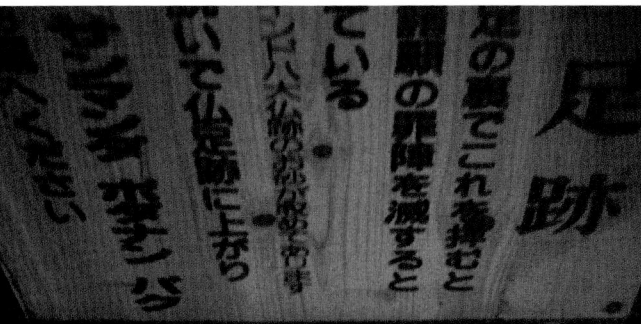

At the Shinto shrine

she bows, lost in the still point

between heaven and earth.

祈り手が

神社でお辞儀

天地の静止

A young woman
presses her hands together
turning smoke into prayer.

手を合わせ
願う女性に
煙舞う

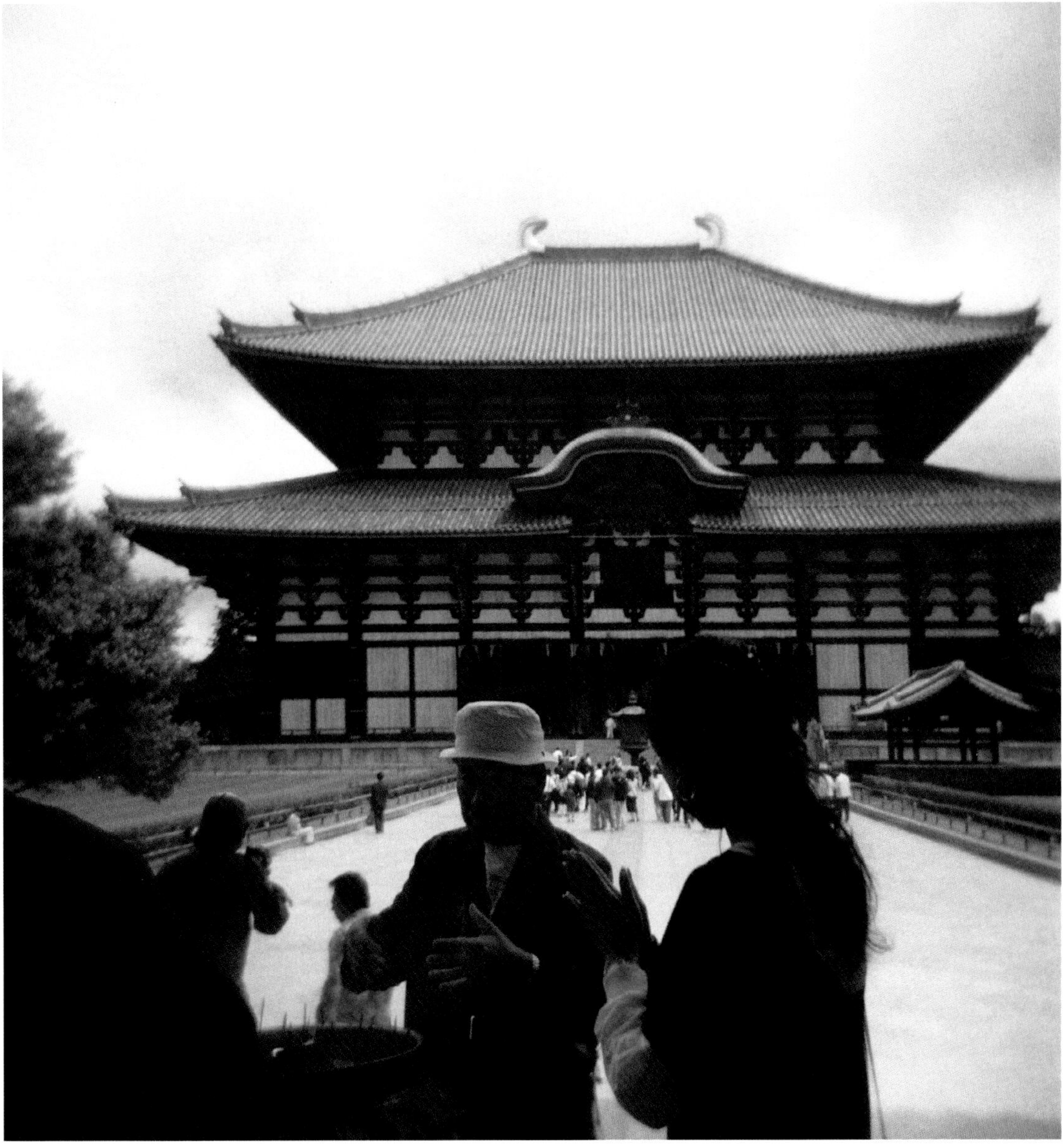

Taste the sweet, ripe plum;
hear the sad *shakuhachi*.
Something stirs within.

甘杏
侘しい尺八
搔き立てる

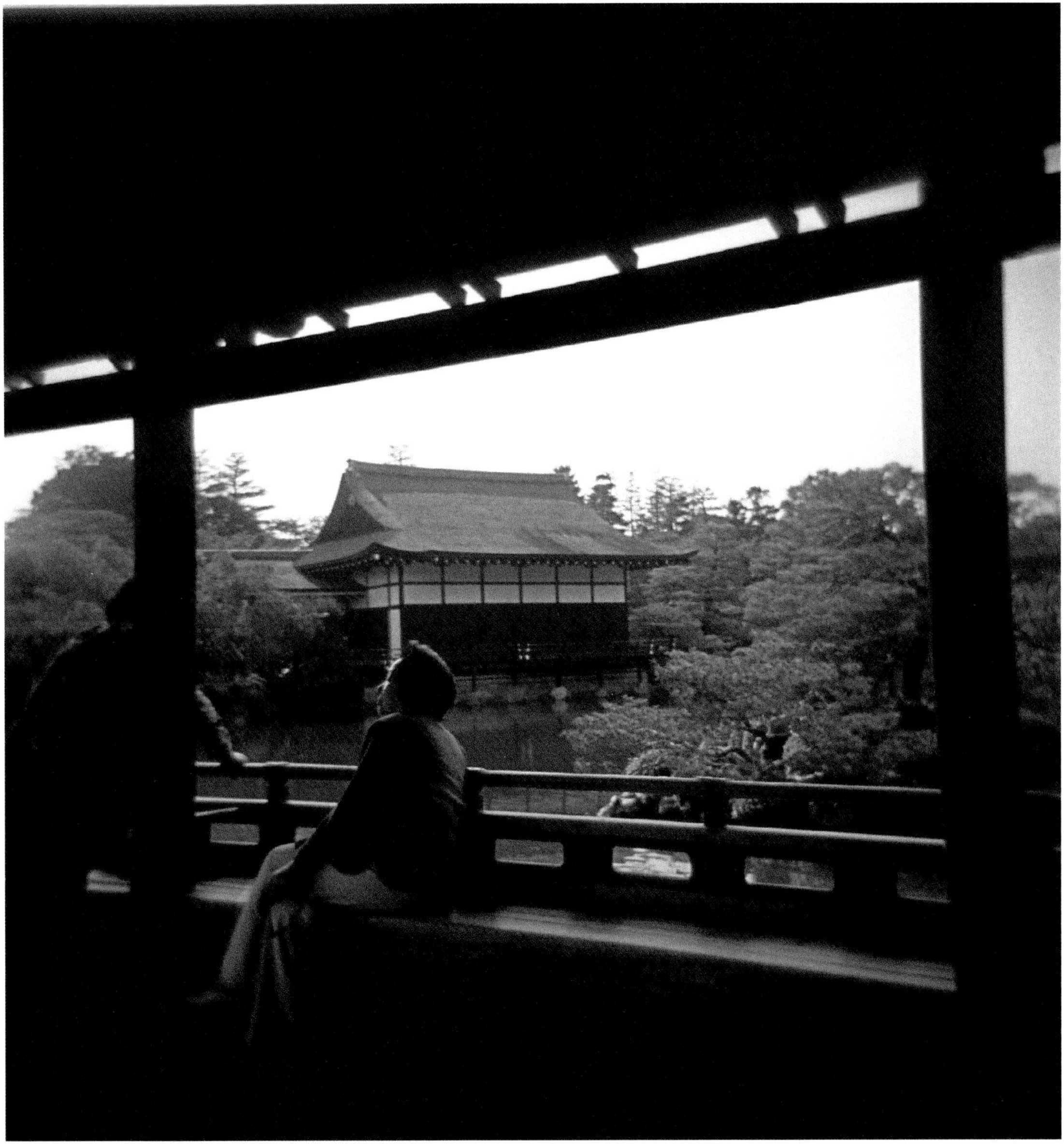

On the garden path
men and women come and go
talking of Bashō.

庭の道
男女が行き来
芭蕉を語る

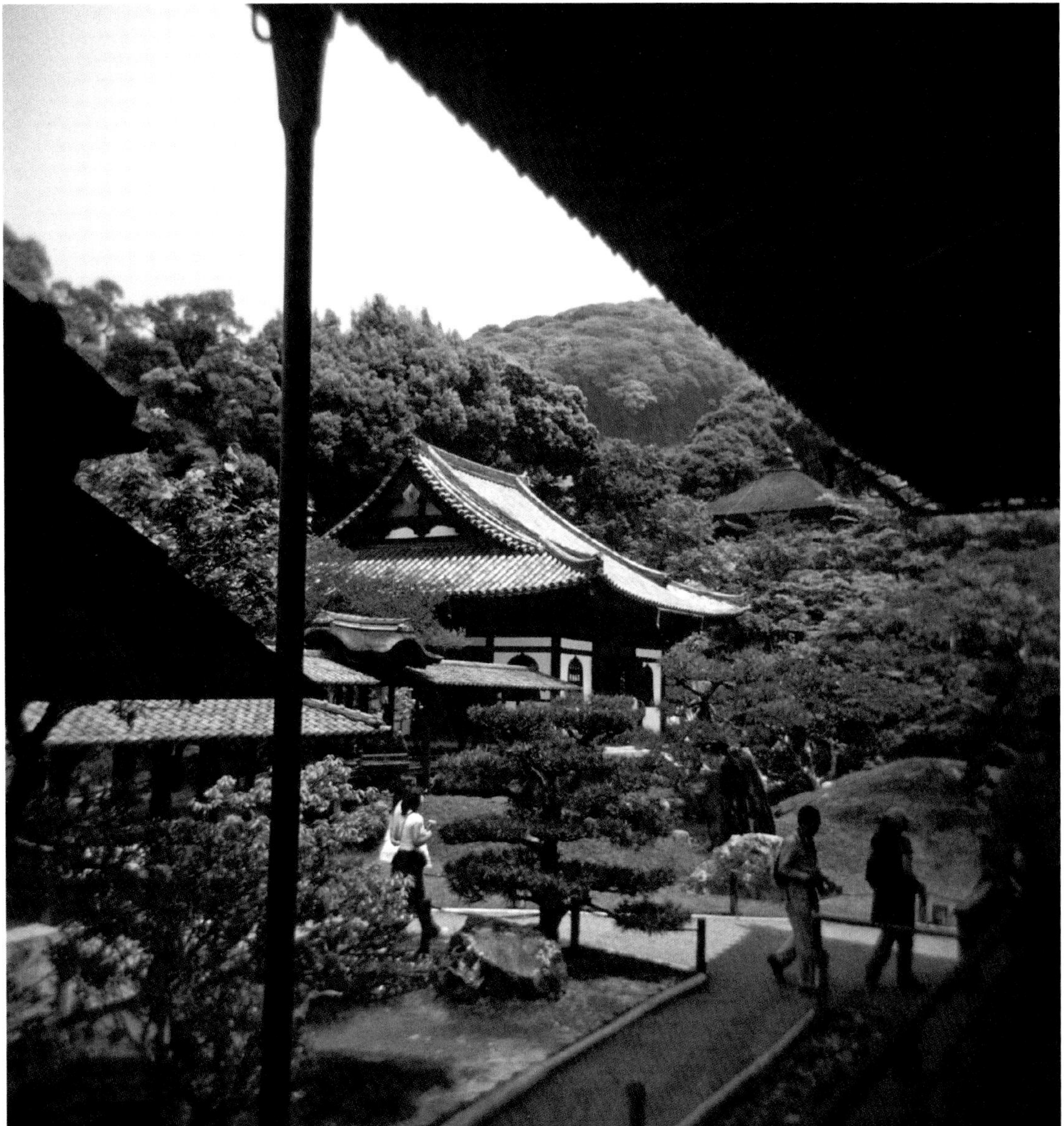

The rice is planted,
the work of the farm stands still,
crows cry with longing.

田植え終え
農家は静か
カラス鳴く

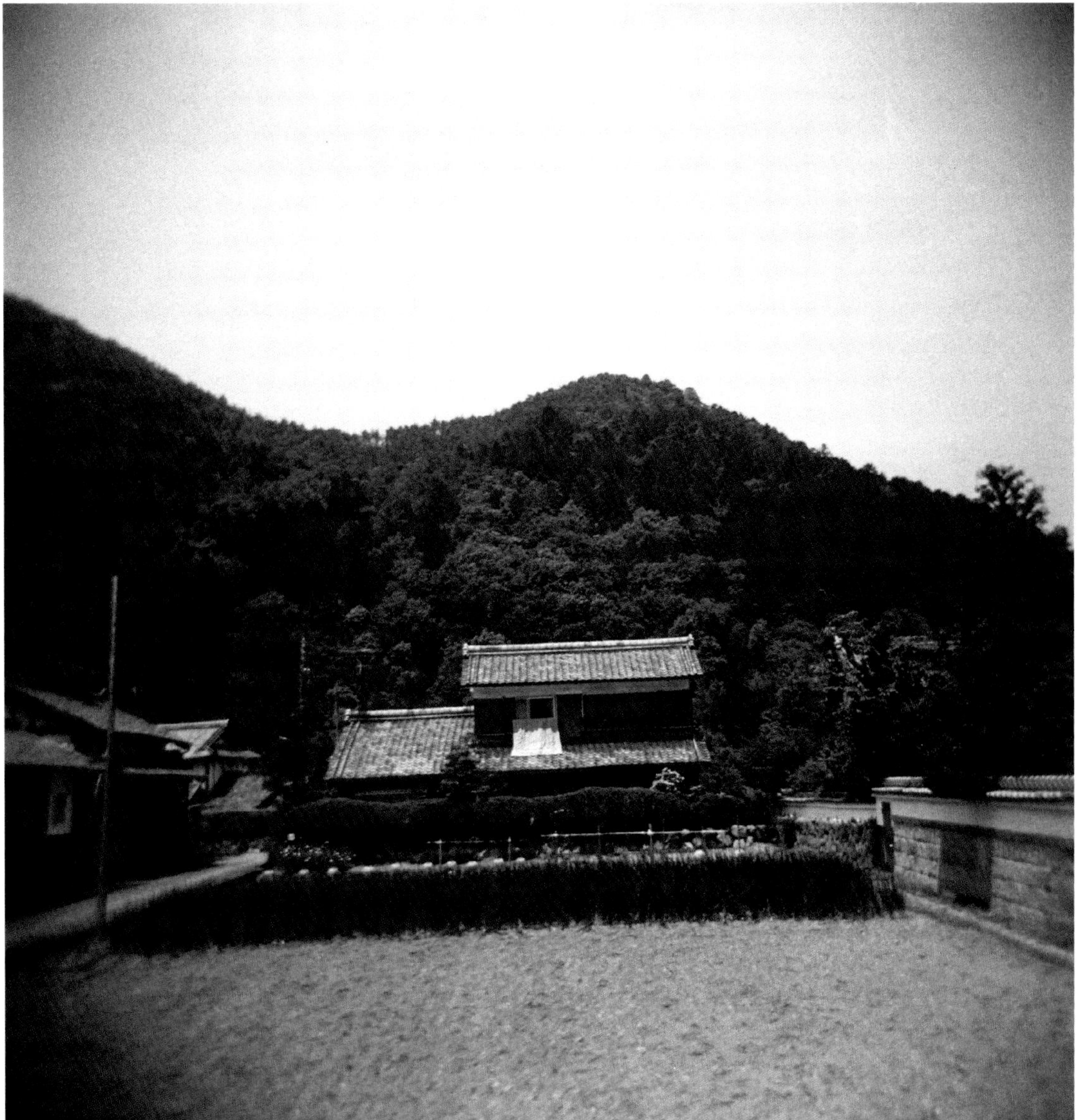

Can you really tell

which is shadow, which bamboo,

walking this lonely path?

影と竹

見分けがつかず

寂れ道

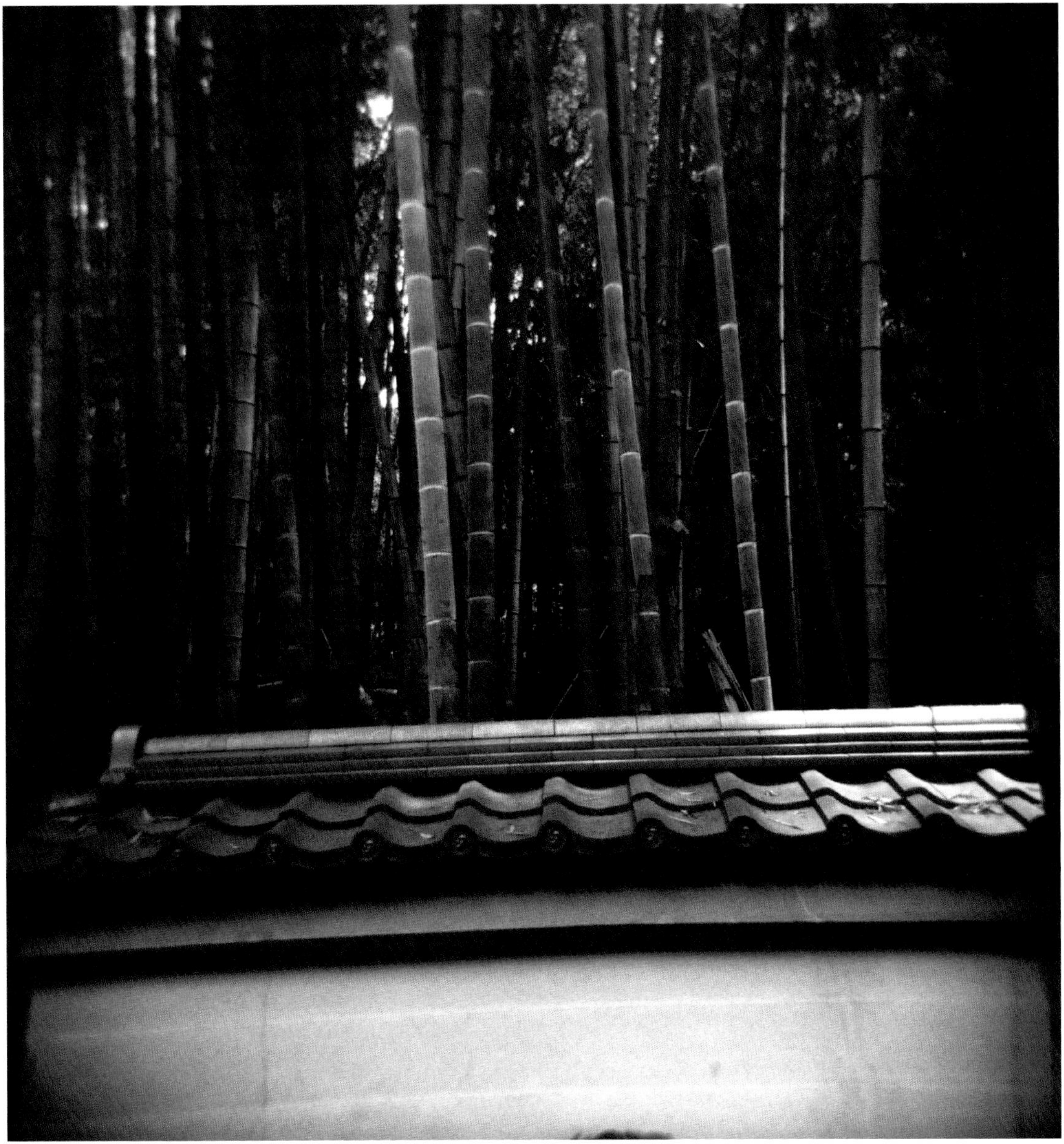

The bamboo forest
the train station's steel beams —
same light, same shadow.

竹林
駅の鉄骨
明りと影

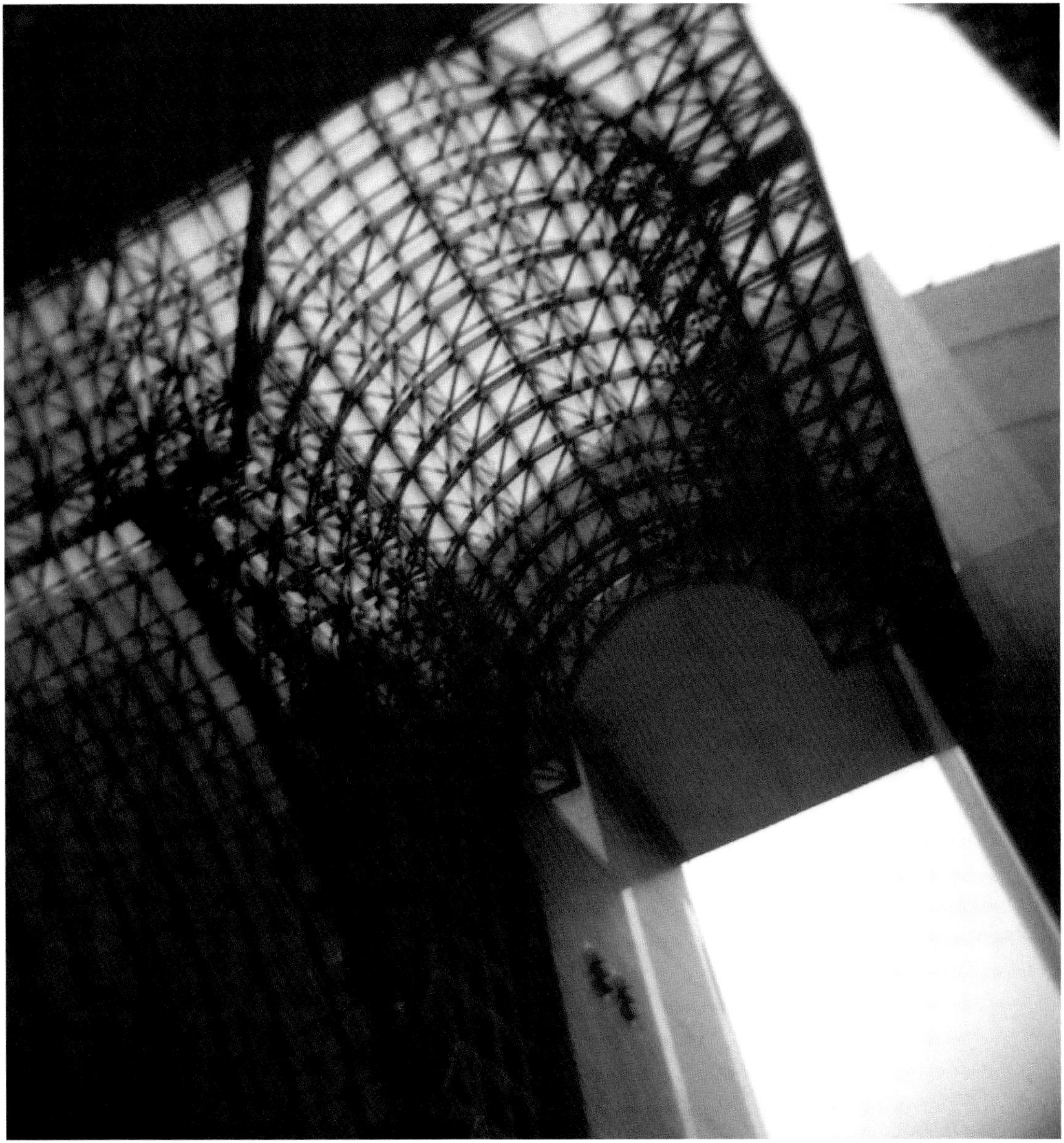

I can't help but note
the faint hint of sandalwood
as she disappears.

彼女去り
ビャクダンの香
かすかに舞う

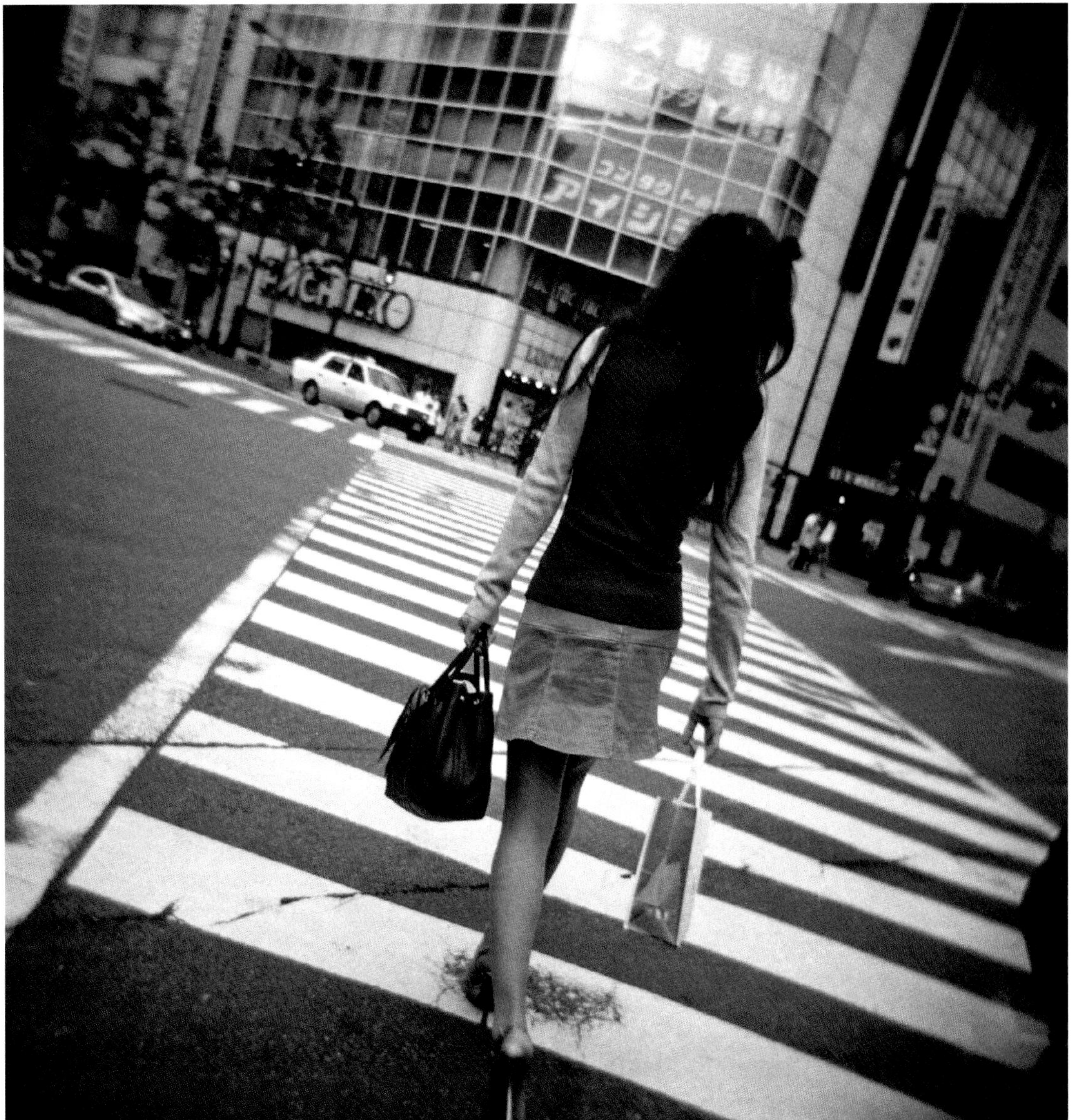

I could have sworn I
saw a hairy dragon fly
there from temple prayer.

私は見た
祈り人から
飛び立つ垂れ髪龍

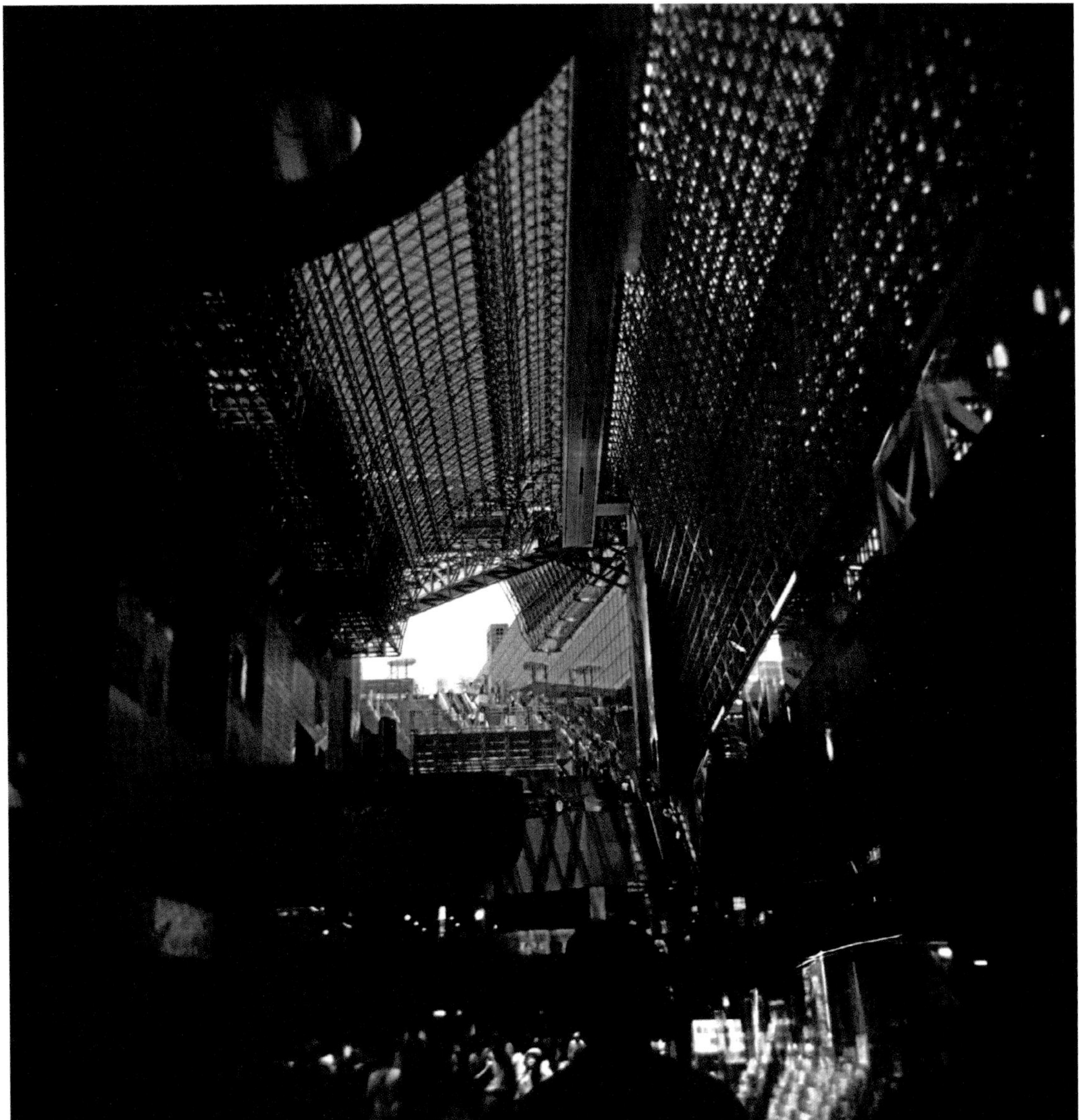

Hiroshima:

Riding the trolley
with no memory of grief
the great wheels turn —
young girls in school uniforms
a man in a black suit.

広島

女学生
背広の男
大車輪
トロッコに乗る
悲しみ知らず

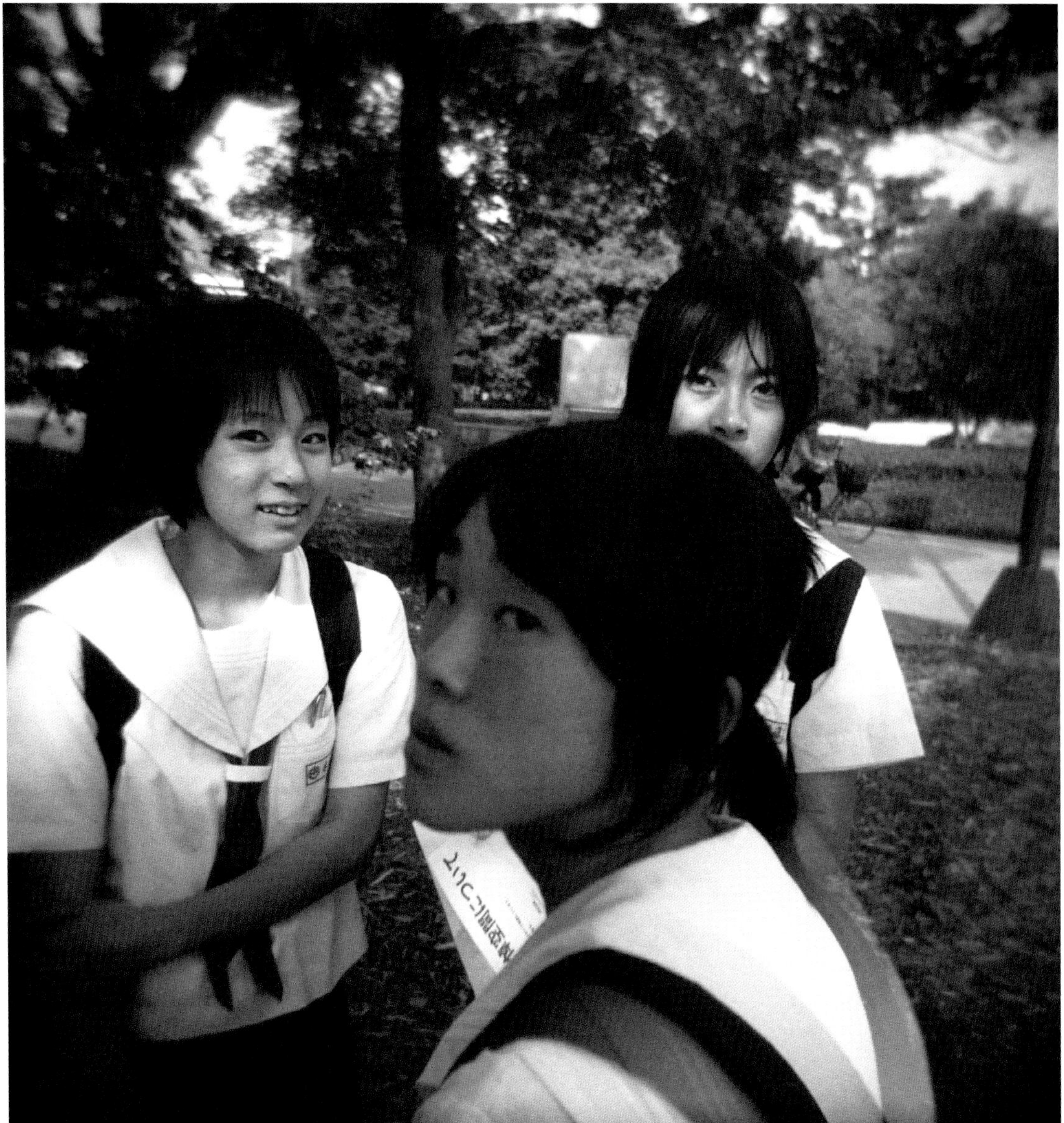

Peace Garden Waka

On the very place
where children turned into dust,
children turn, unsure
still of where the lilies bloom
or how many cranes to fold.

平和庭園の和歌

この場所で
塵となった
子らは知らず
ゆり咲く場所と
折られる鶴を

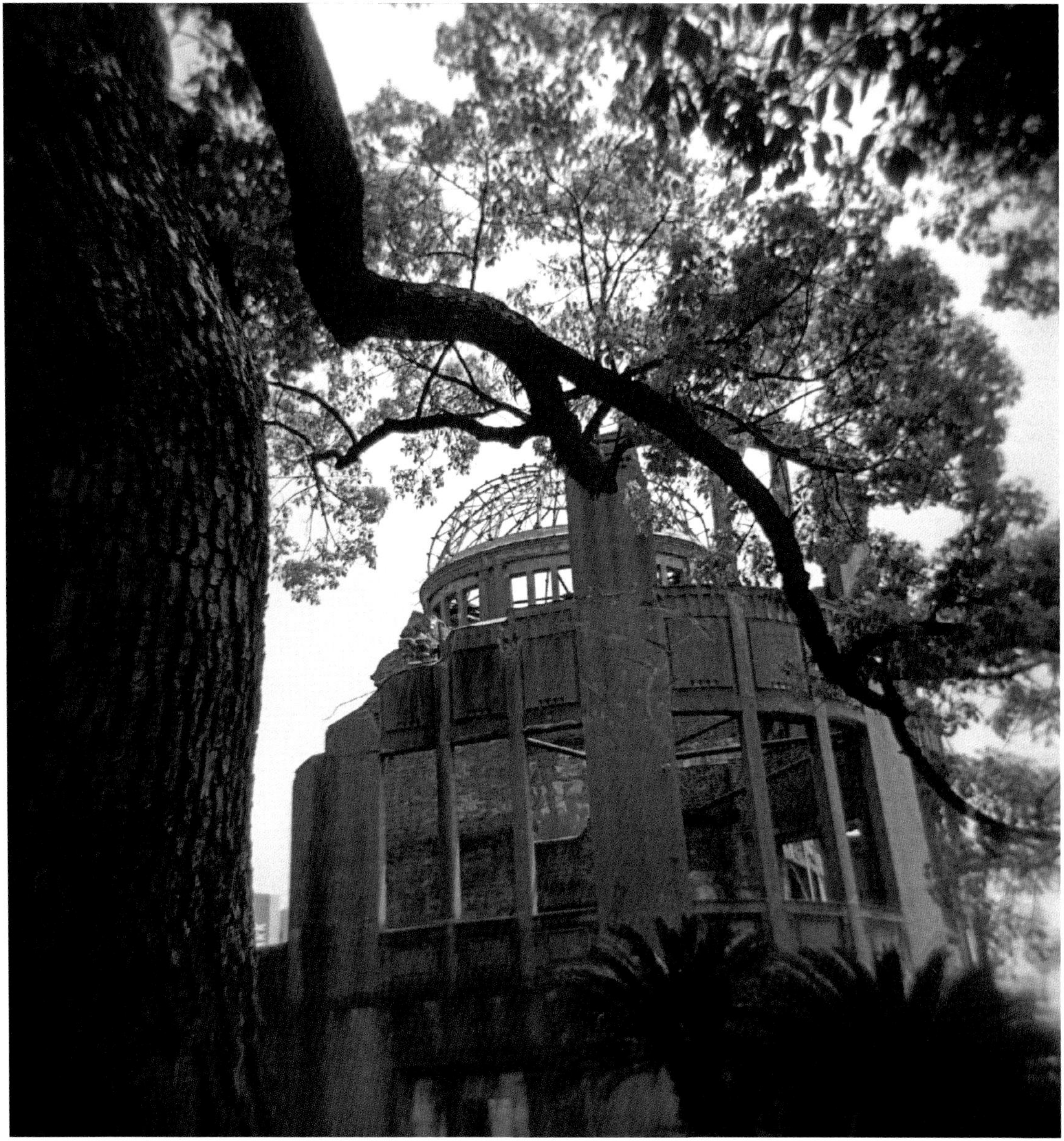

What does this tell you —
Hello Kitty has replaced
the Bodhidharma?

ハローキティ
菩提達磨
の代わりに
置かれてる
一体何を
意味することか

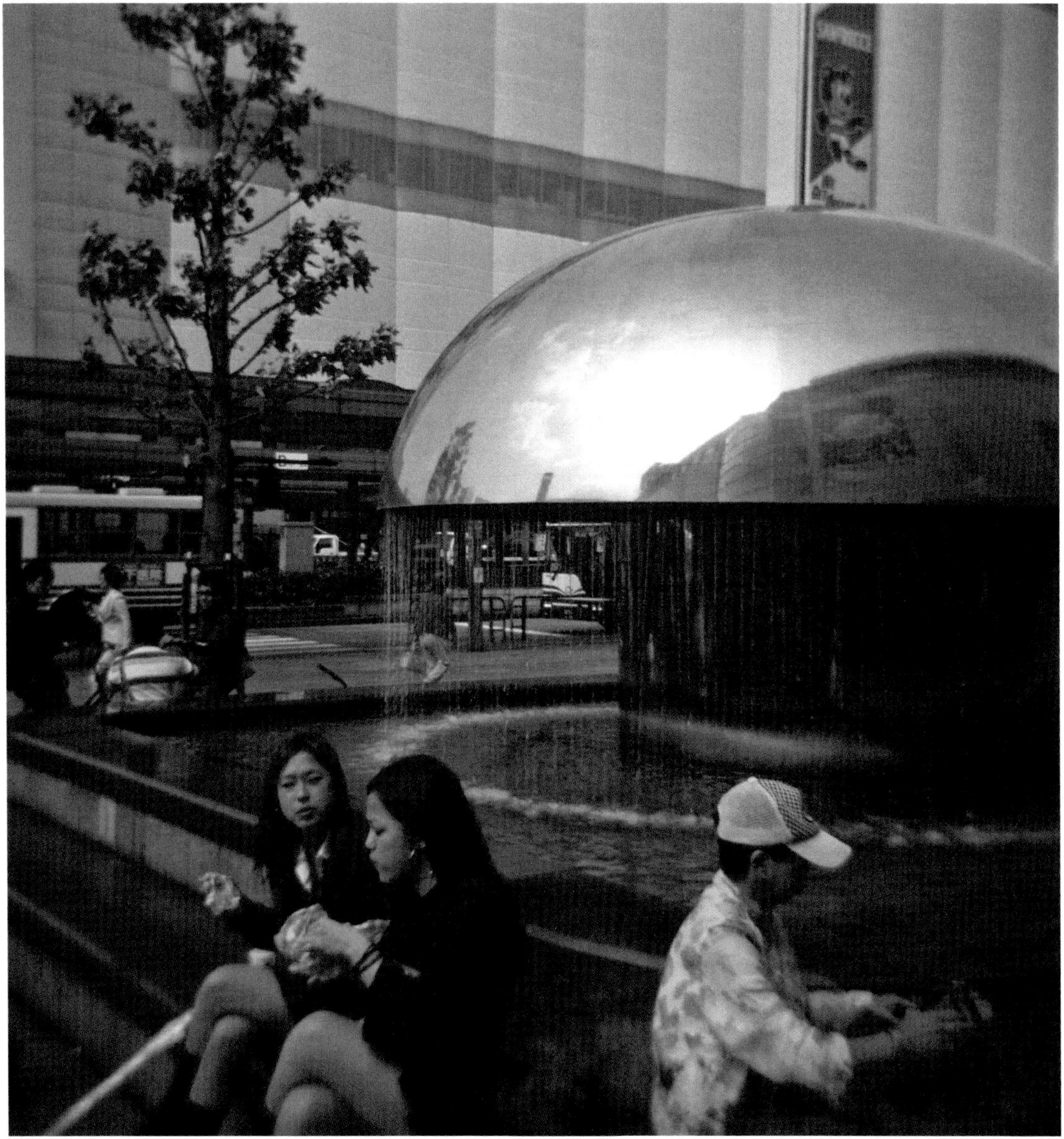

These affairs of ours,

such important business.

Like cigarette smoke.

重要な

僕らの仕事

煙草の

煙のように

An empty wine bottle —
someone got happy.
Are they still, now?

空っぽの
ワインボトル
幸せに
誰かがなった
まだ幸せか

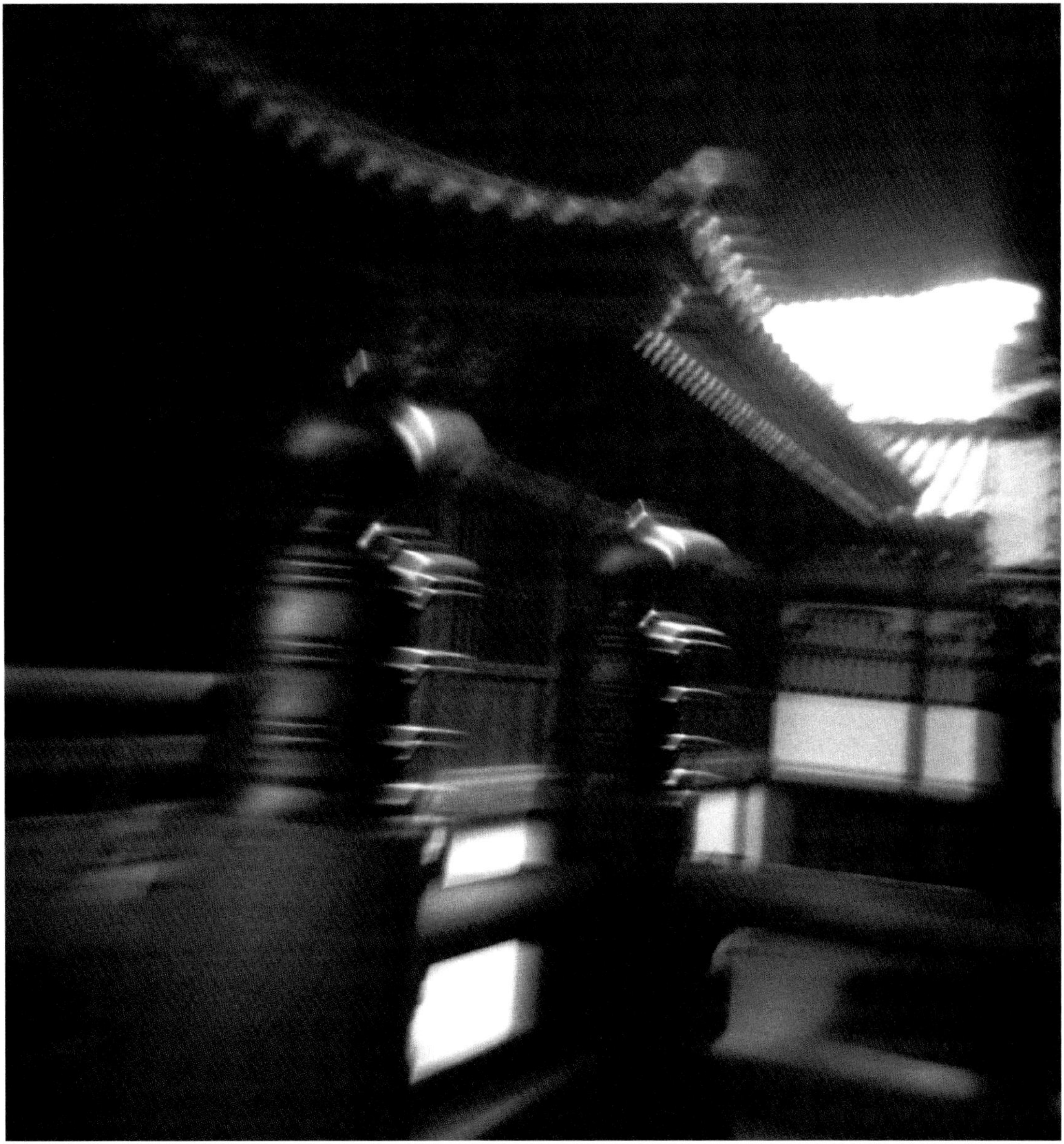

Smoke from cigarettes,

sandalwood from morning prayer,

what is the difference?

何が違う

朝の祈りの

ビャクダンと

煙草から

漂う煙

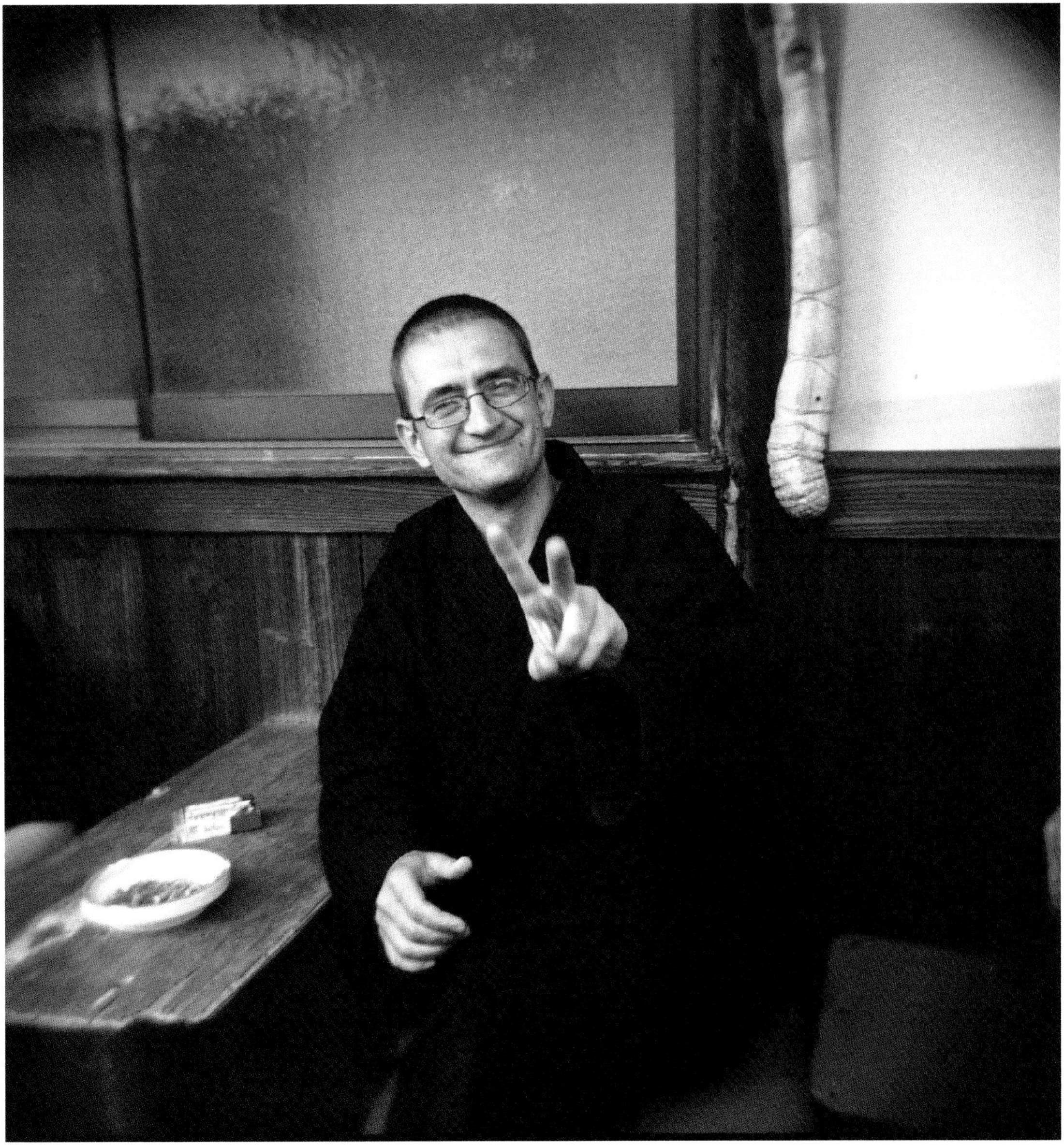

"Engrish" Found Poem

Mano restaurant:
"Relaxation, Intelligence,
Infinite dream."

「英語」で書かれた詩

真野食堂
「くつろいで、知性豊かに
無限の夢」

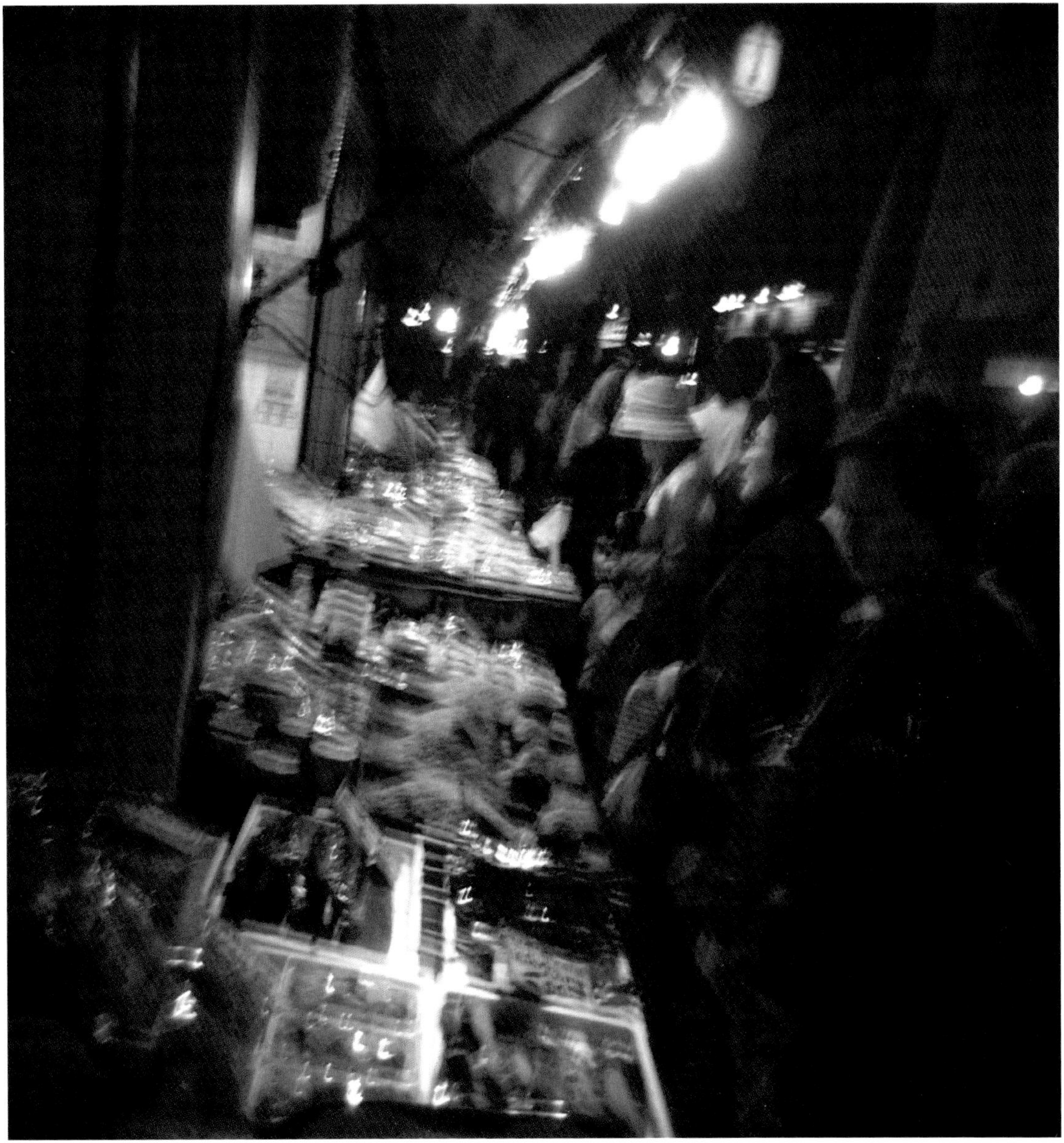

Found Poem:

見つけた詩

ドアを引き、
前進しよう
一度出で
直進しよう
柱の数字
3を押し
開くを押して
ドアを押し
前進しよう

"You pull a door toward you, and
    please advance.
You go out once, and
    please straight.
A button of a number sticks to a pillar,
    at first please push 3 buttons.
Please push open next.
You push a door, and you advance."

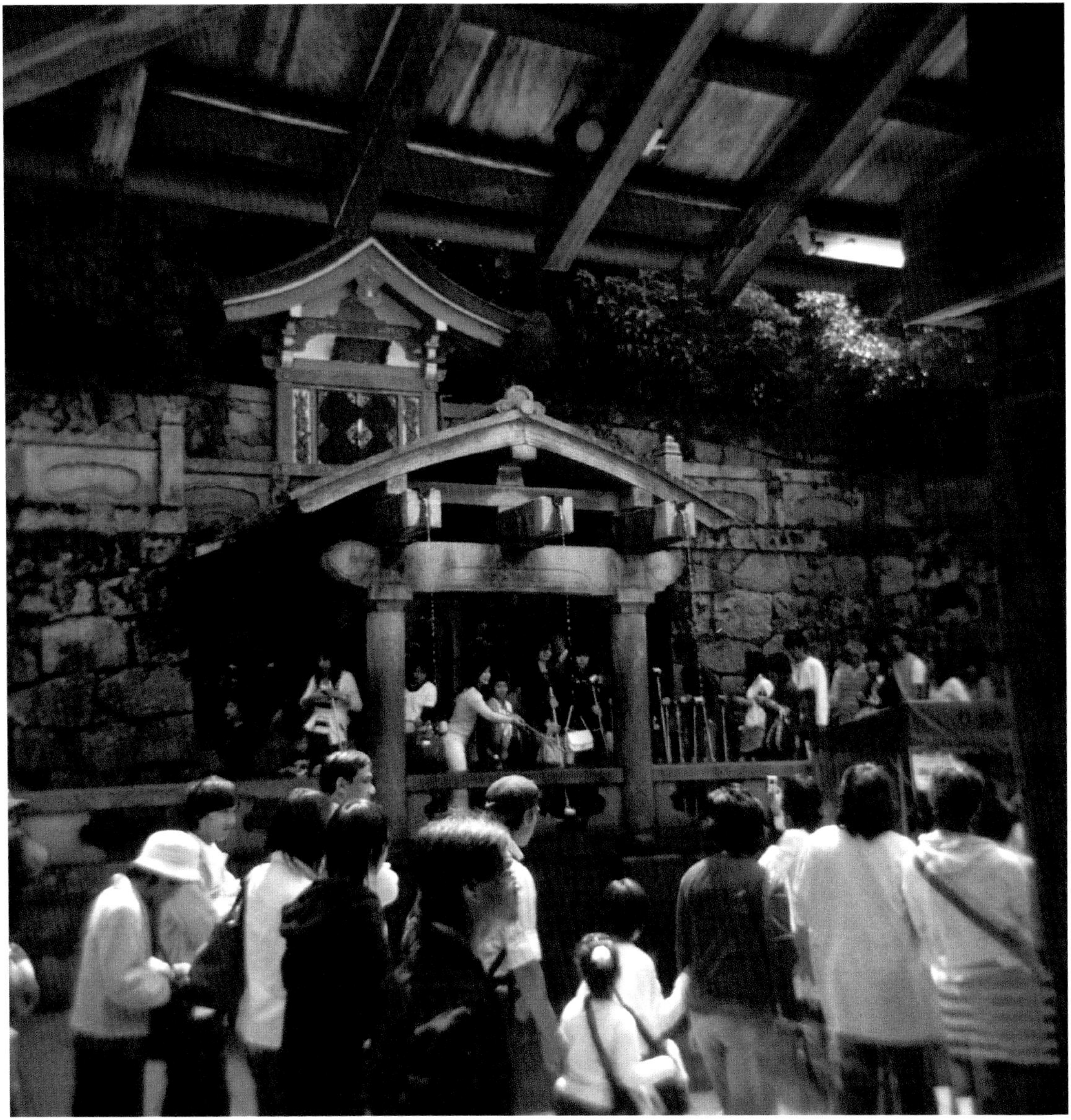

Azalea blooms fall,

lotus flowers fill the pond.

One sits down, one stands up.

つつじ散り

蓮が咲く池

座るものあり

立つものあり

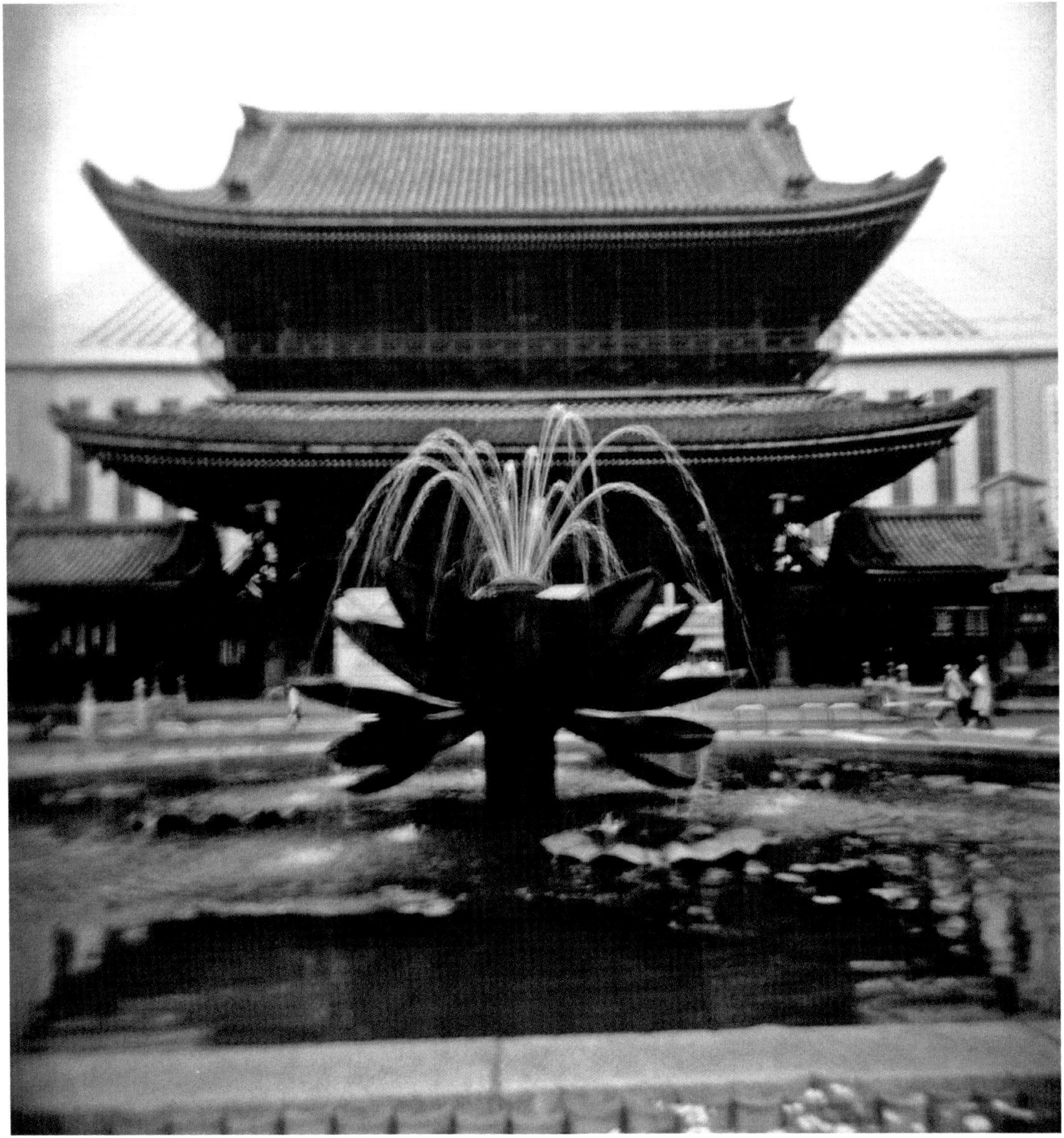

Buddha, like Jonah,
in the ribbed orange belly
of the great stupa whale.

仏様
ジョナのように
オレンジの
クジラの腹に
いるみたい

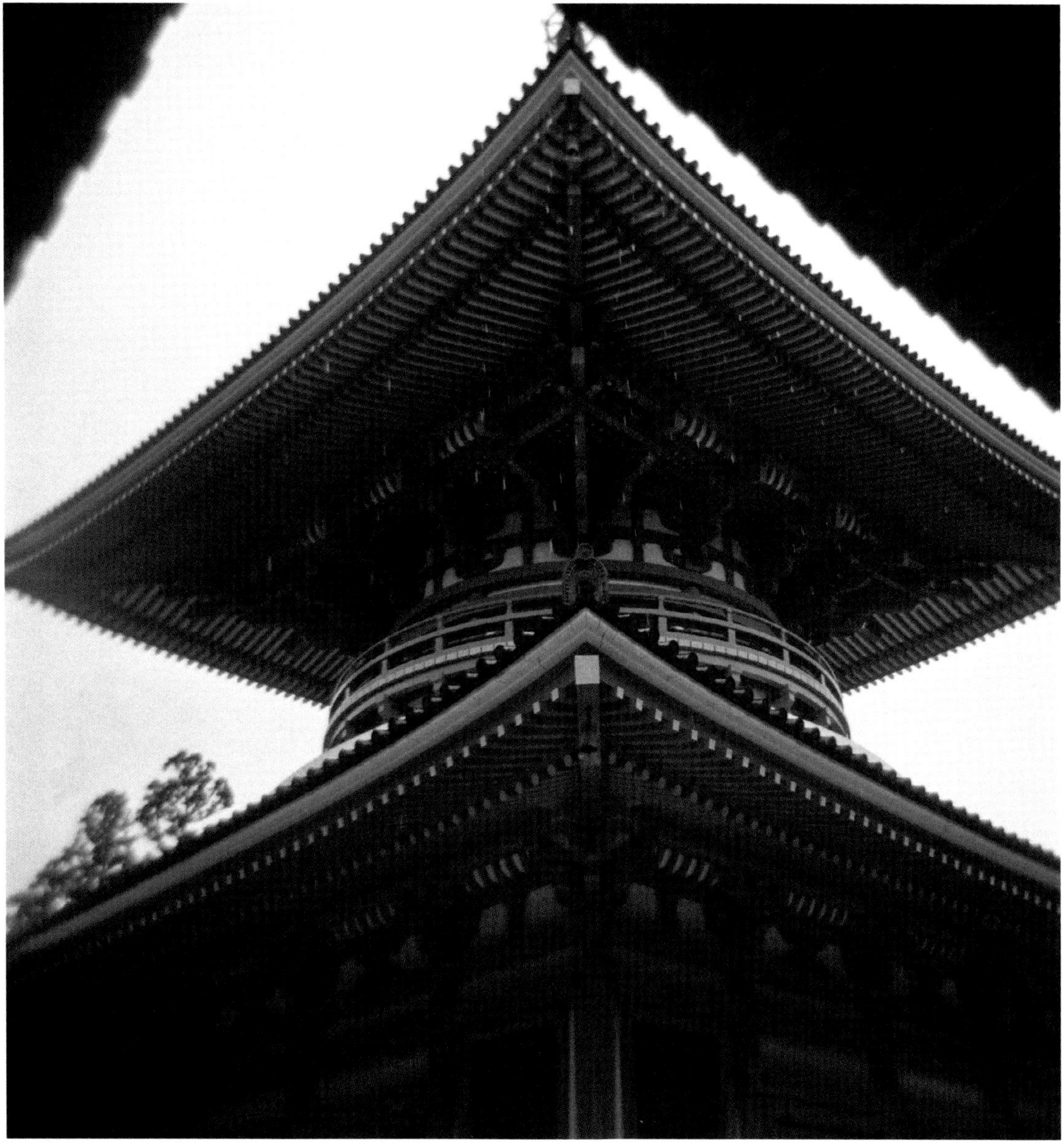

Nishi Honganji

Priests pray sutras
as old men light incense sticks.
What is the smell of prayer
in the Pure Land?

西本願寺

老人が
蝋燭つけて
僧侶らが
経を読む
浄土の祈り
香りはいかに

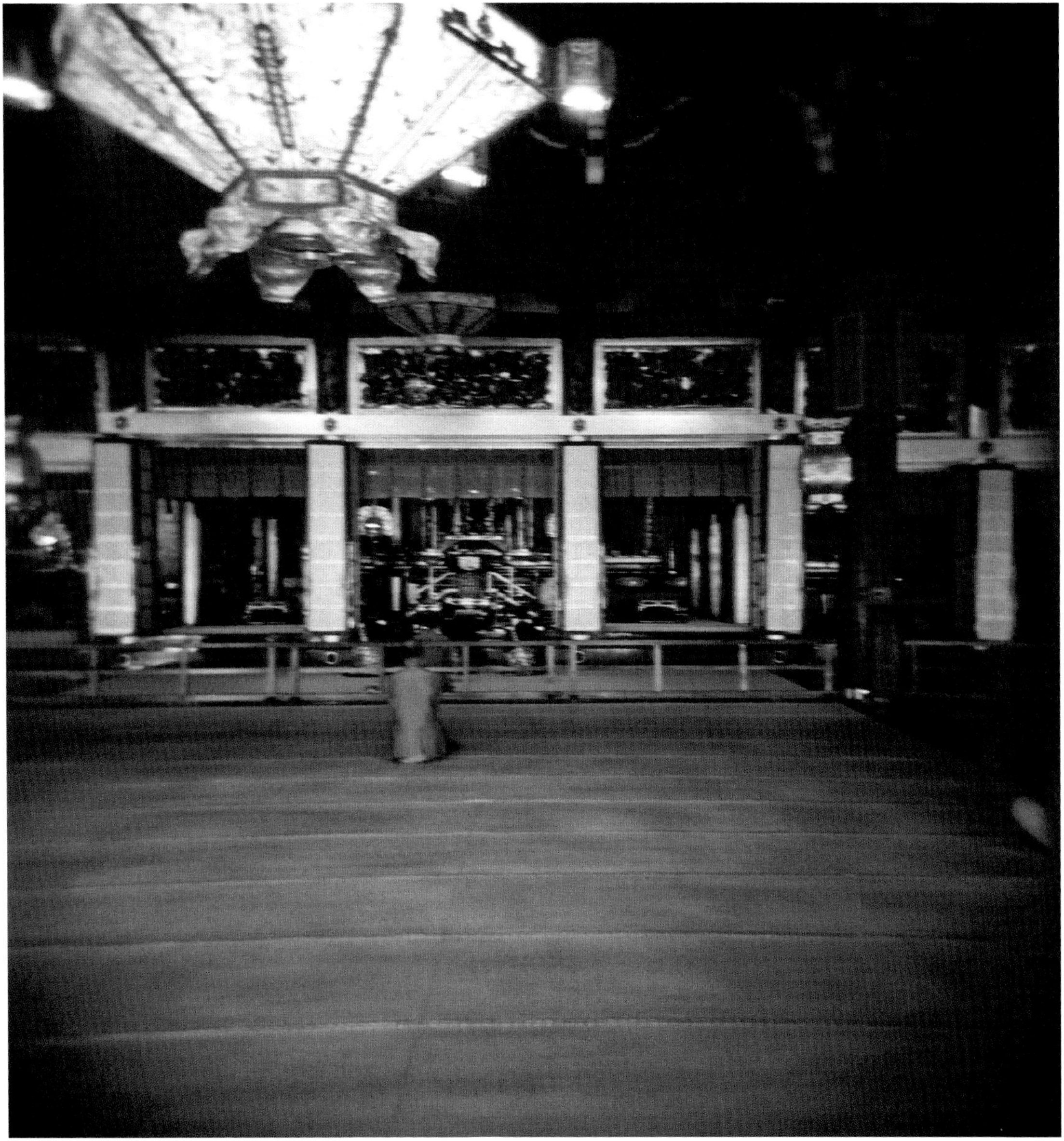

Rikshah wheels turn,
rose petals fall in the rain —
a monk plays with fire.

人力車輪動き
バラの花びら
雨に散る
　一人の坊主
火で遊ぶ

当宝秘仏不動明王護摩供修法所

Kinkakuji

Blue heron, beak up,
still among the blue iris,
feet deep in the mud.

金閣寺

青い鷺
あやめの中で
嘴上げる
ぬかるみに
深く立つ

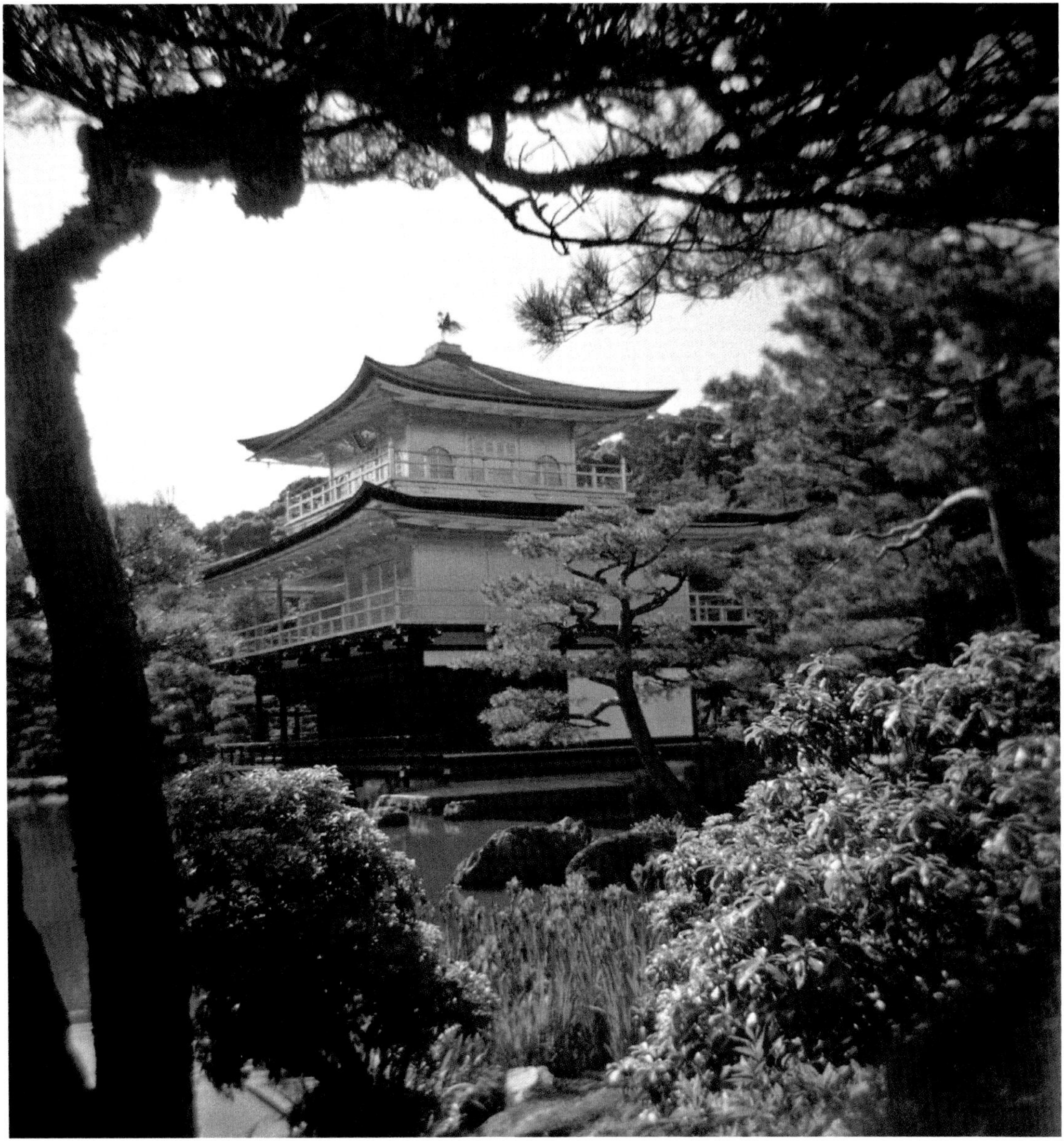

Sit. Be still, awake.

Here are mountains and forests

rising from deep seas.

座って

静かに目を開ける

深海に

そばだつ森林

ここにあり

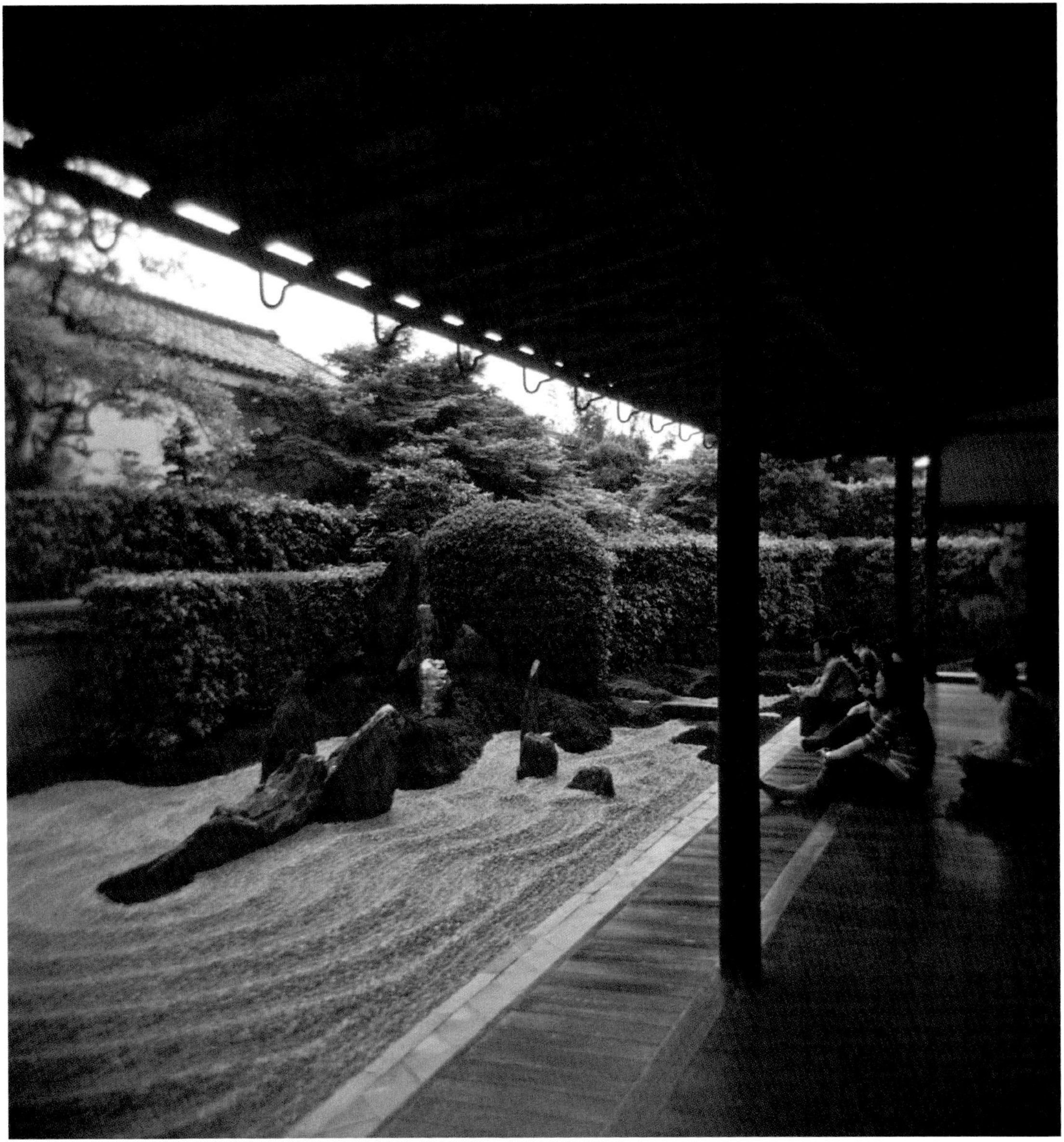

Temple Flute (Shakuhachi)

Where is the music —
in the wind breathed through the flute
or the hearer's mind?

尺八

この音は
どこから来るの
聞く人の
心の音か
フルートの音

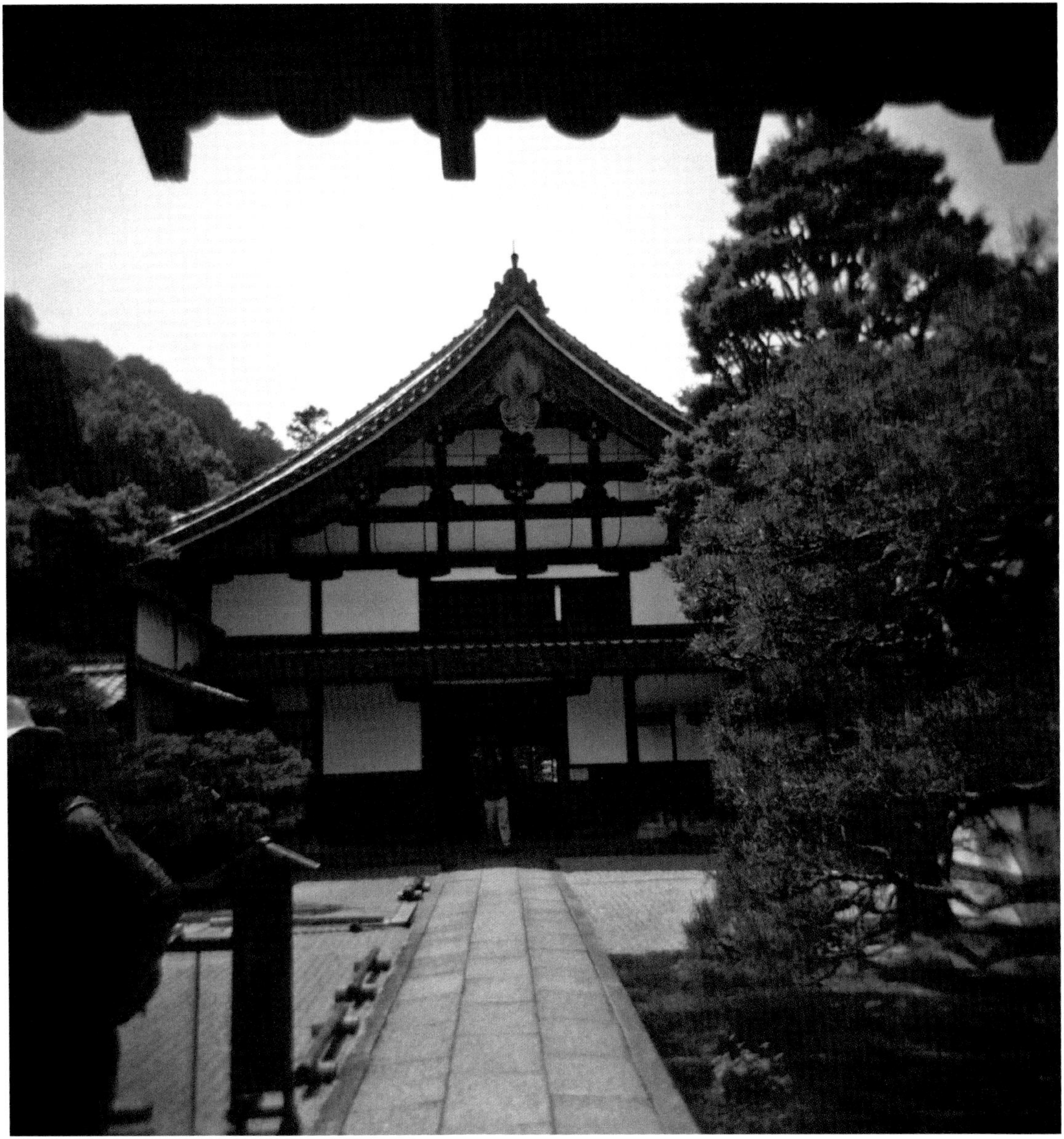

In the Master Hall

High above, dragons fly.
What is it about dragons
that I would join them?

マスターホール

空高く
龍が飛ぶ
私もともに
飛べるかな

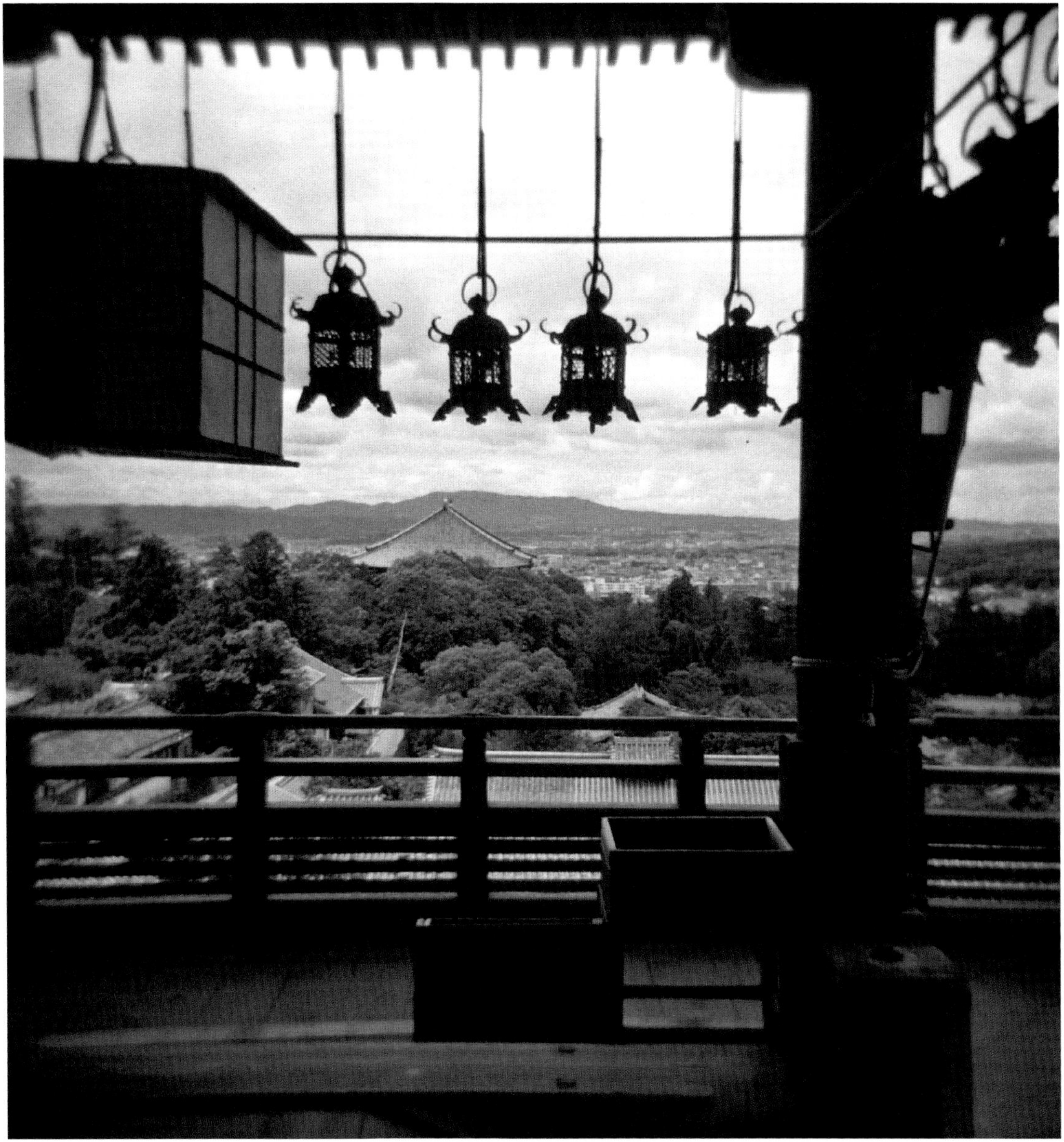

This temple will fall

before the great pine lays down

its last cone in prayer.

この寺は
最後の松の実
落ちる前
崩れるだろう

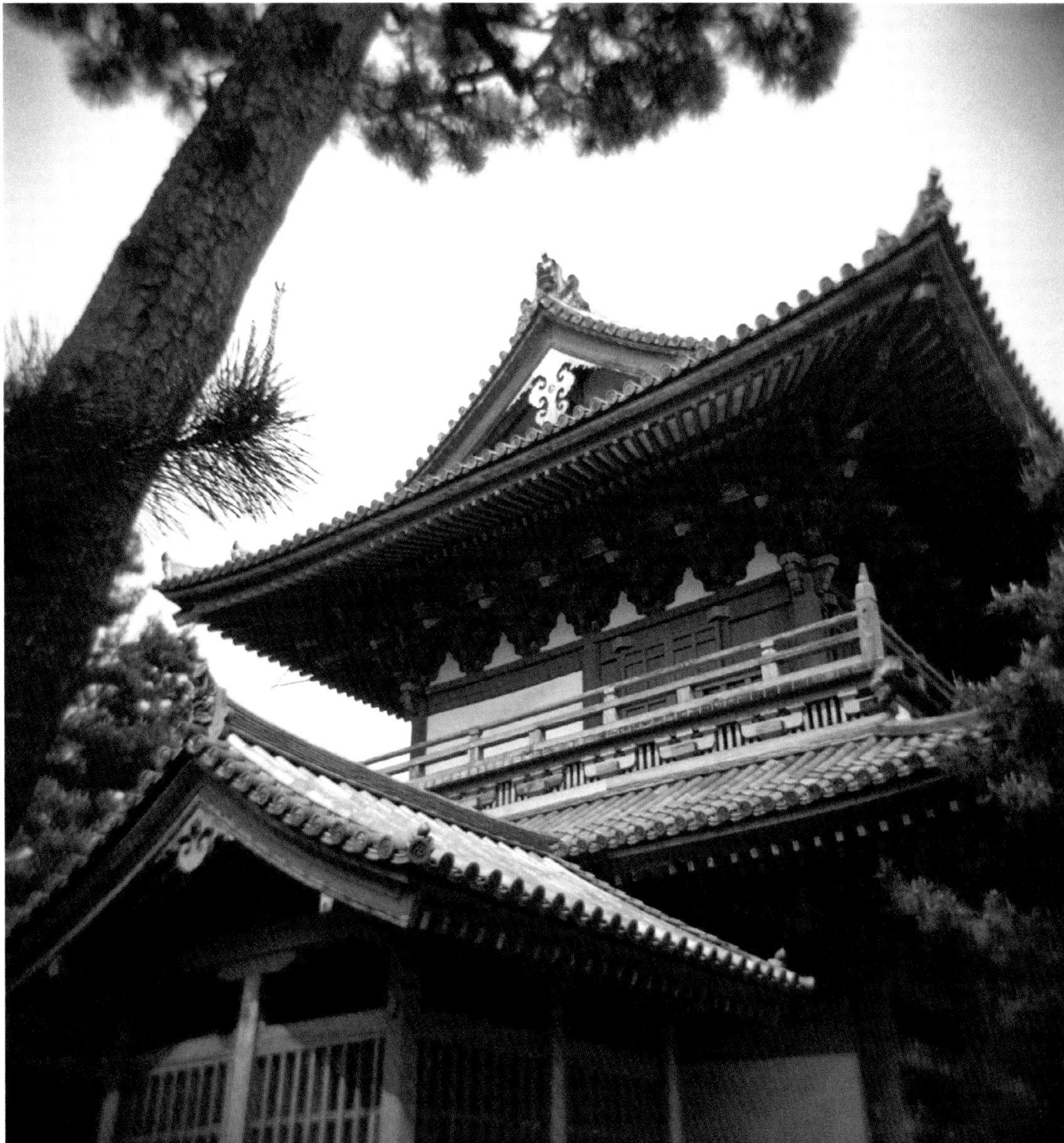

If you look closely

you can see Bodhidharma

walking toward the gate.

近くに行けば
会えるかも
門へと歩く
菩提達磨

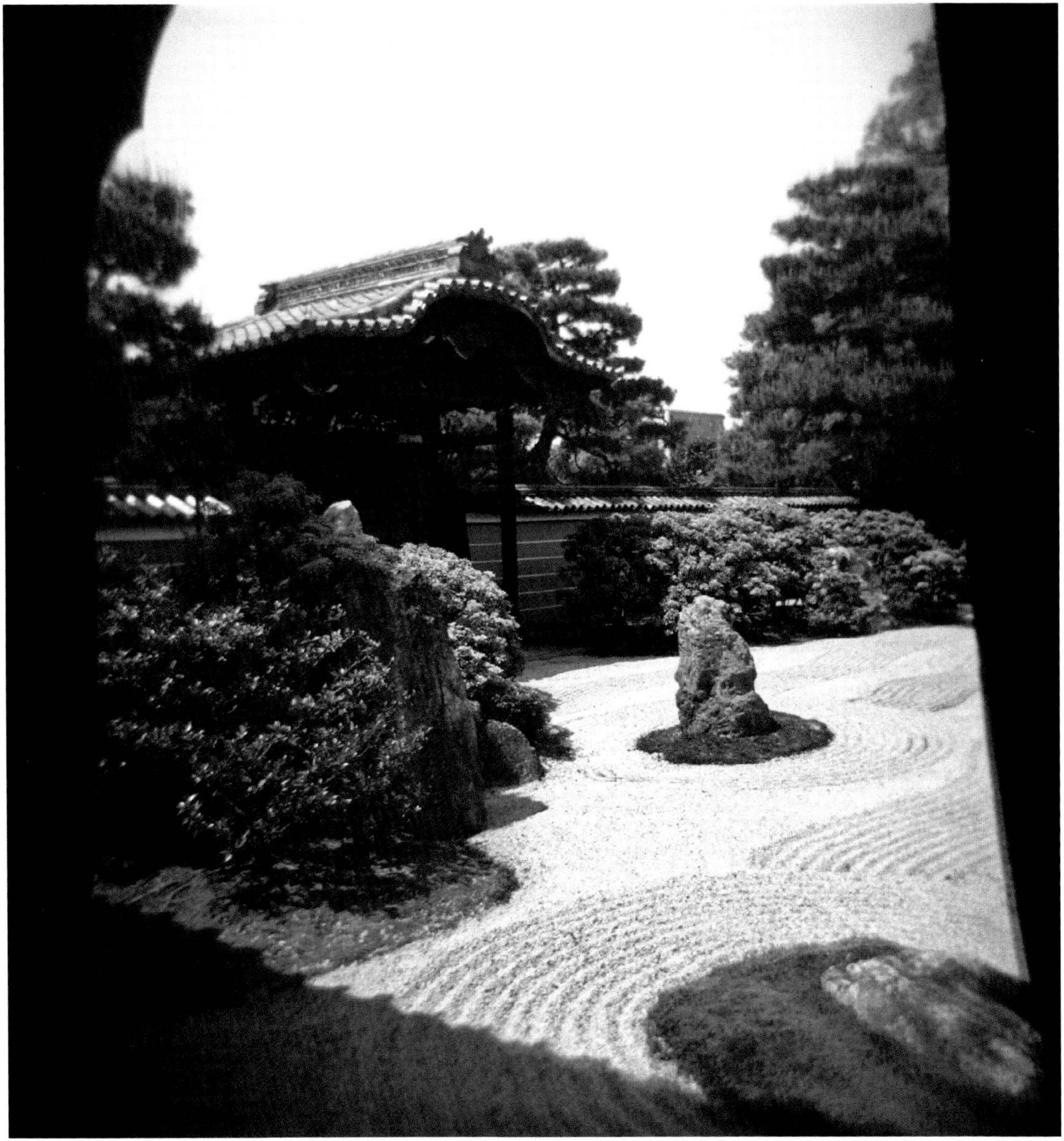

I am rock and sand,

the mountains and all seven seas,

dust of every star:

fifteen rocks in raked, white sand

within peeling stucco walls.

僕は岩

砂と山々

星屑と

七つの海だ

剥がれた

しっくい壁に

15の岩と

白い砂

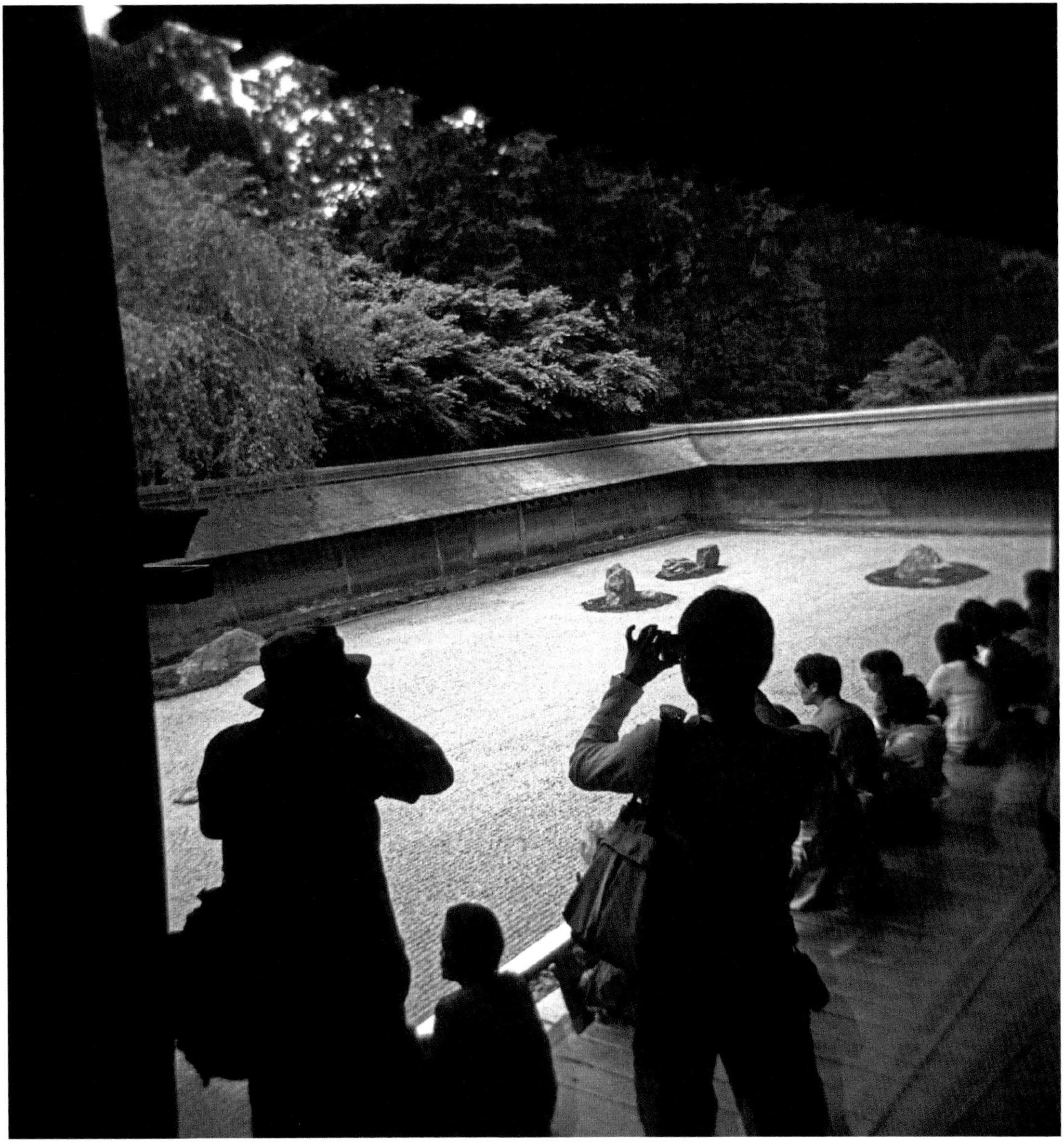

Zazen

Such concentration —
only consider the small,
busy, gray spider
practicing meditation
by spinning his web.

座禅

座禅中
考えるのは
忙しく
巣を駆け回る
灰色の小蜘蛛

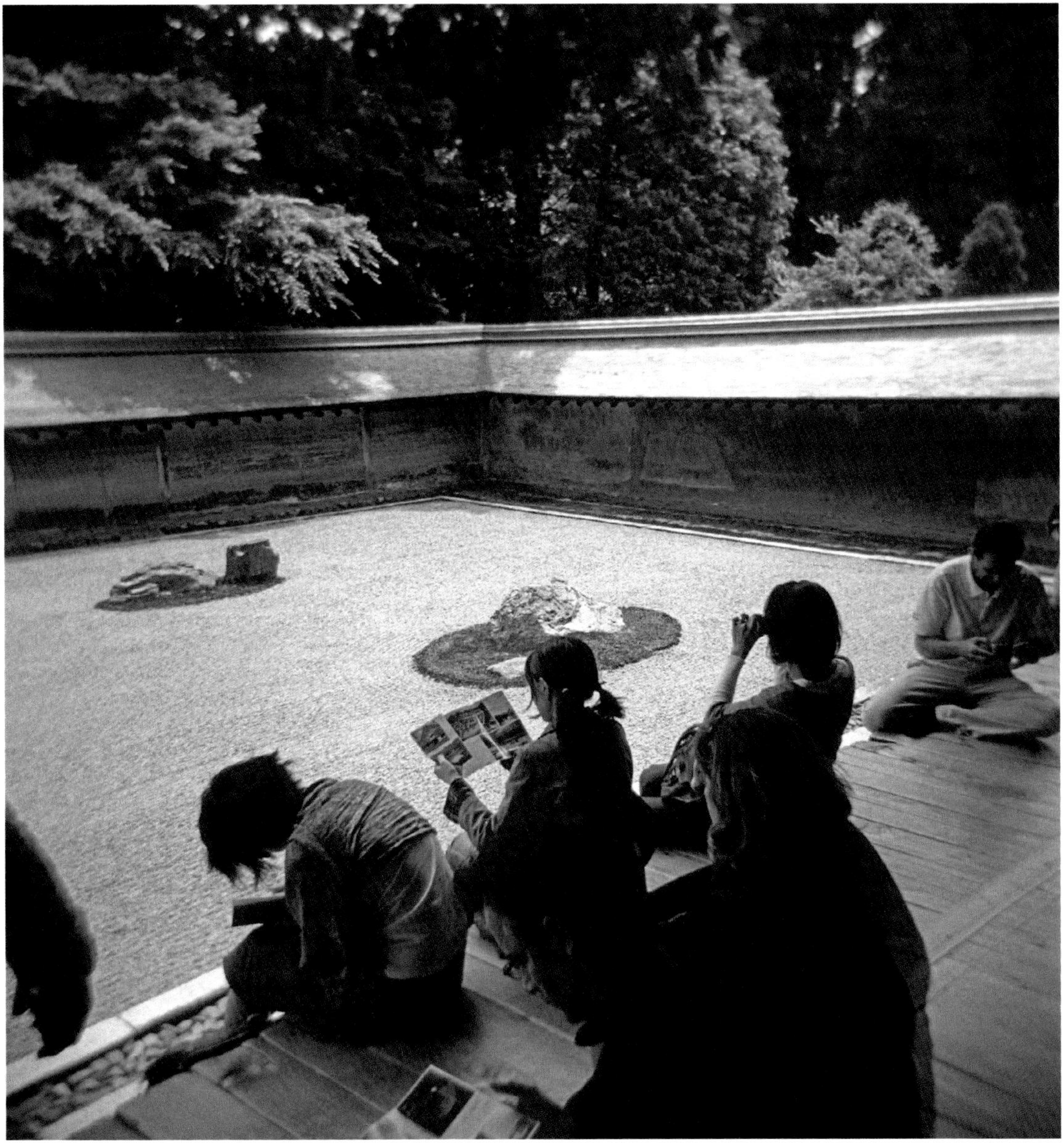

Monks ran to prayer
dragons flew to the rafters —
tourist stands alone.

祈り手へ
僧らが走り
たるきへと
龍が飛んだ
旅人が
一人立つ

Daishoin, Miyajima

The seeker swings the
ancient beam, the great bell tolls,
the bibbed *jizo* smile.

宮島の大聖院

坊主らが
大鐘鳴らす
前掛け着けた
地蔵が笑う

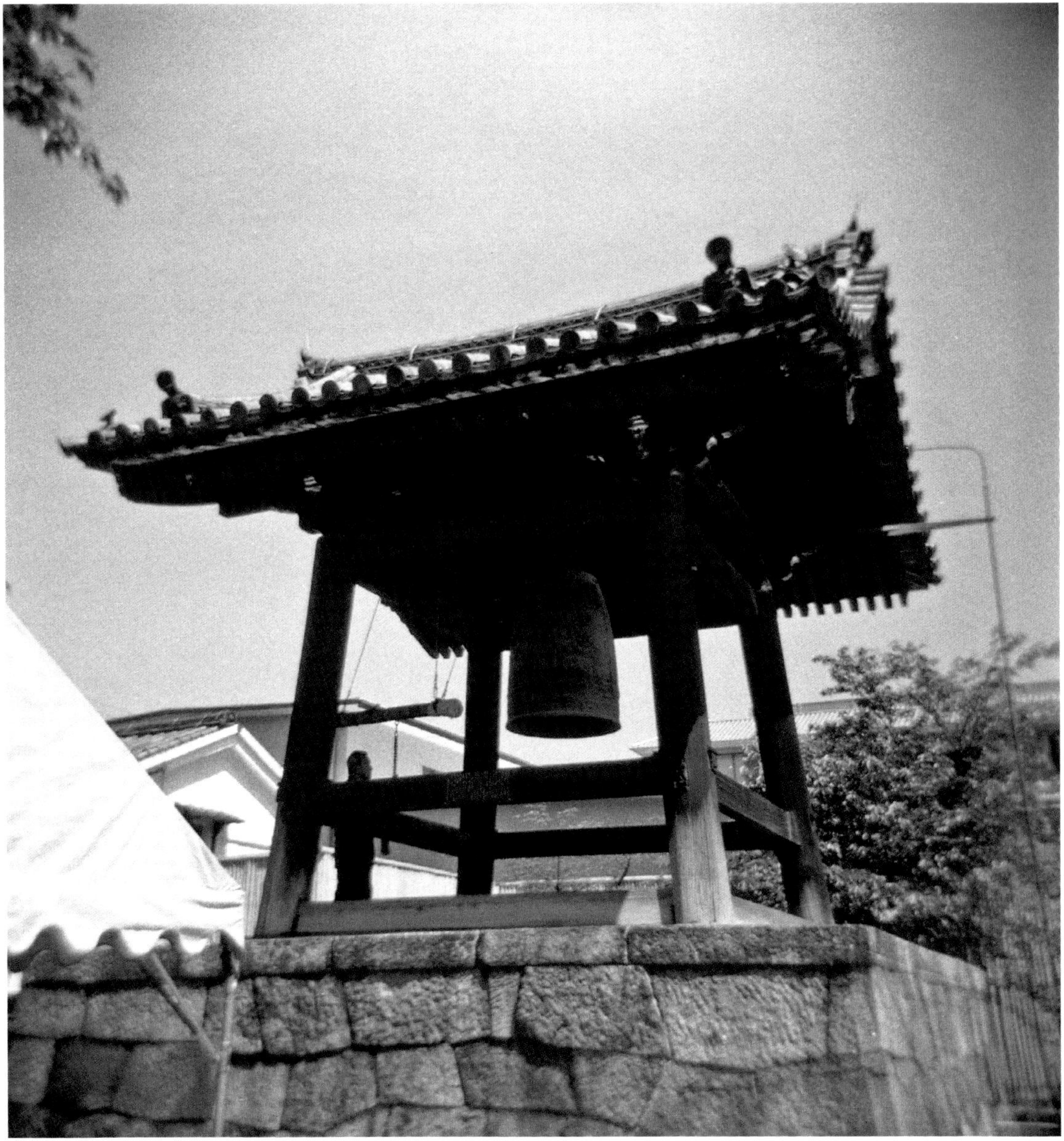

Flower of the well

water drawn at six a.m.

home of the tiger.

井戸の花

6時に水汲む

虎の家

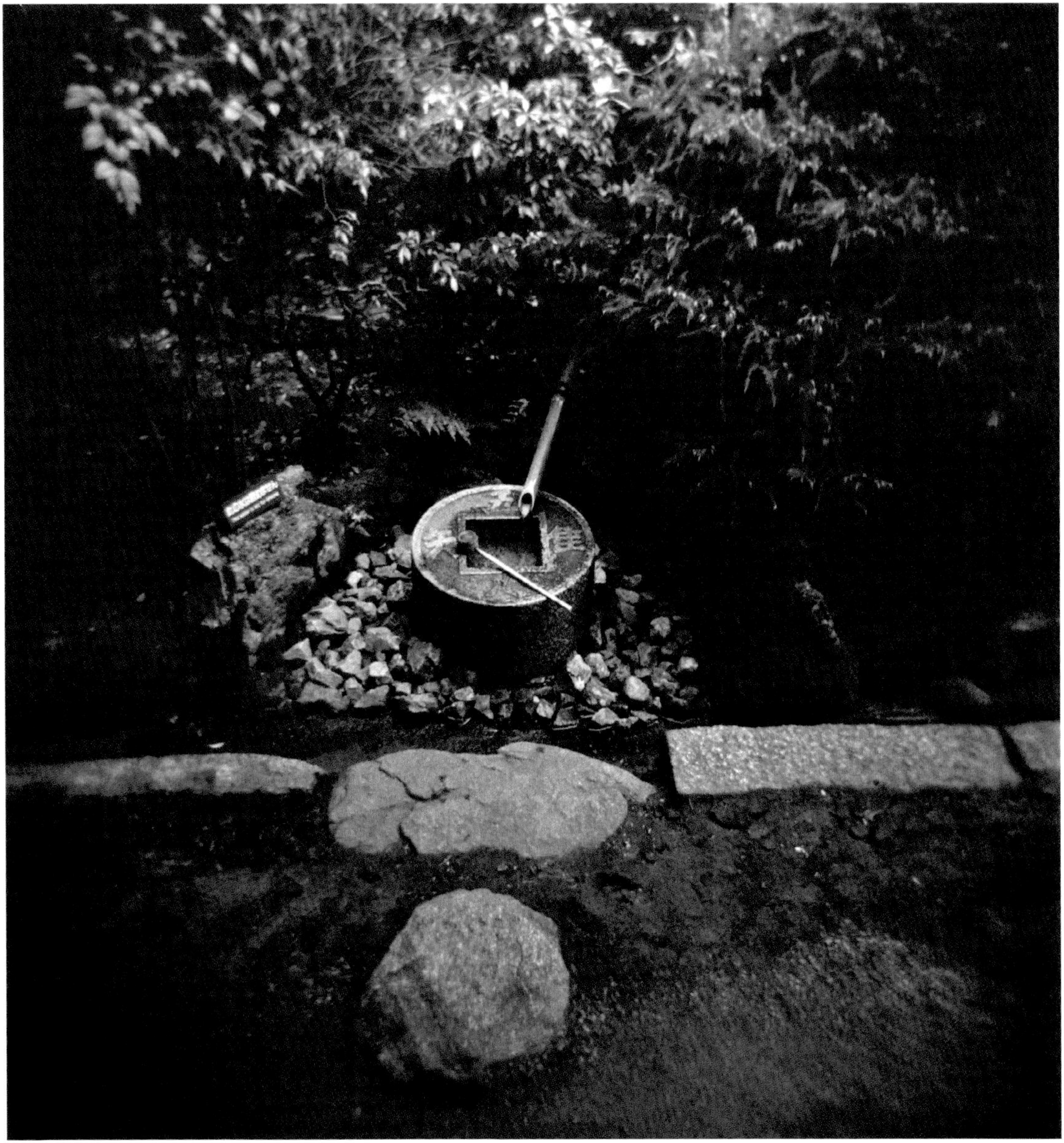

Peering down into

the pool: something I can't see

keeps making ripples.

淵の中を覗込

何かが見ない

漣を立てる

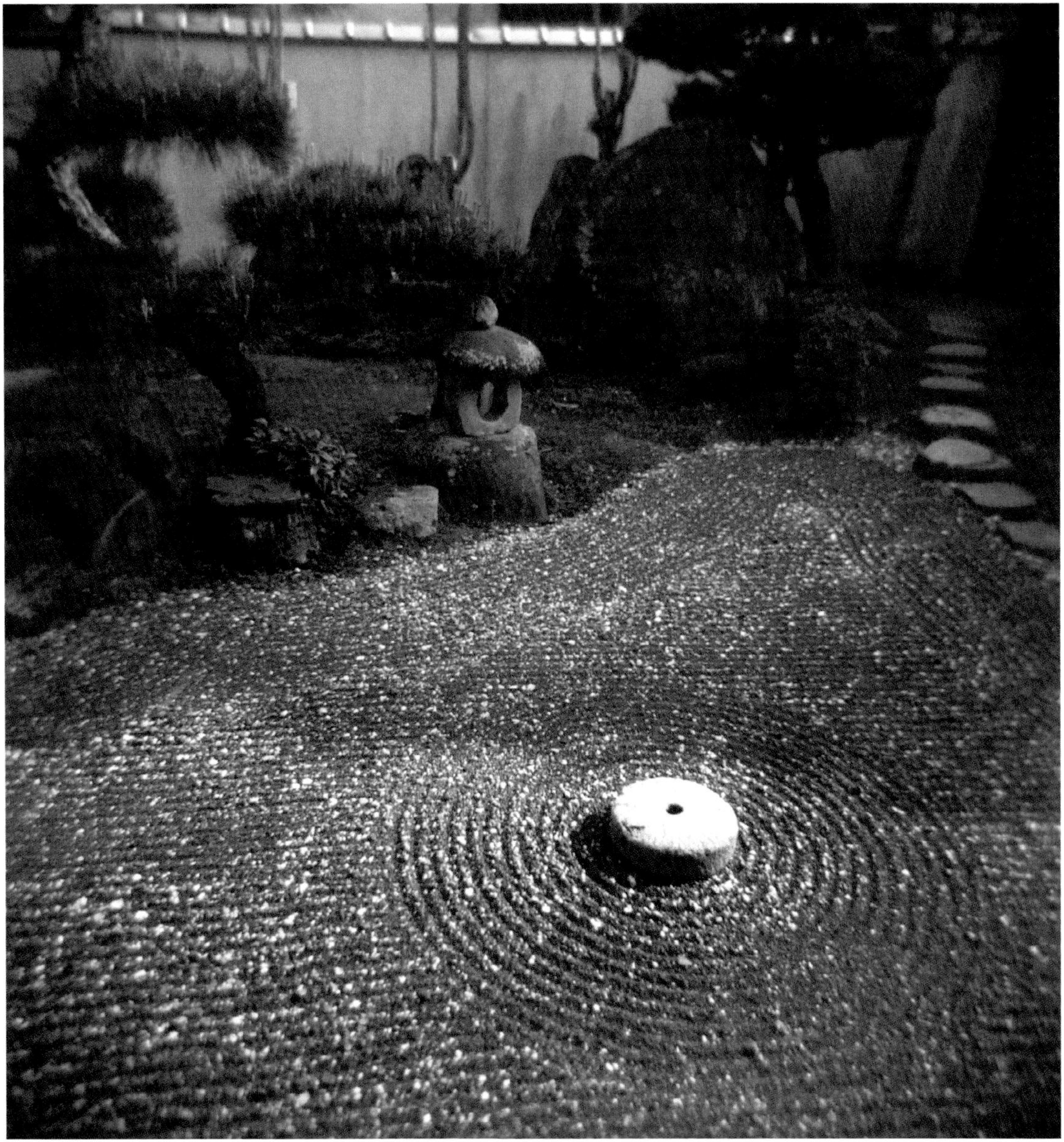

Roshi

The *han* has spoken.
Sitting still in great silence —
sound of compassion,
the sound of mountain graveyard,
the sound of the frog's old pond.

老師

沈黙に
静かに座り
板が話す
情けの音
山の墓地の音
古池に飛ぶ
蛙の音

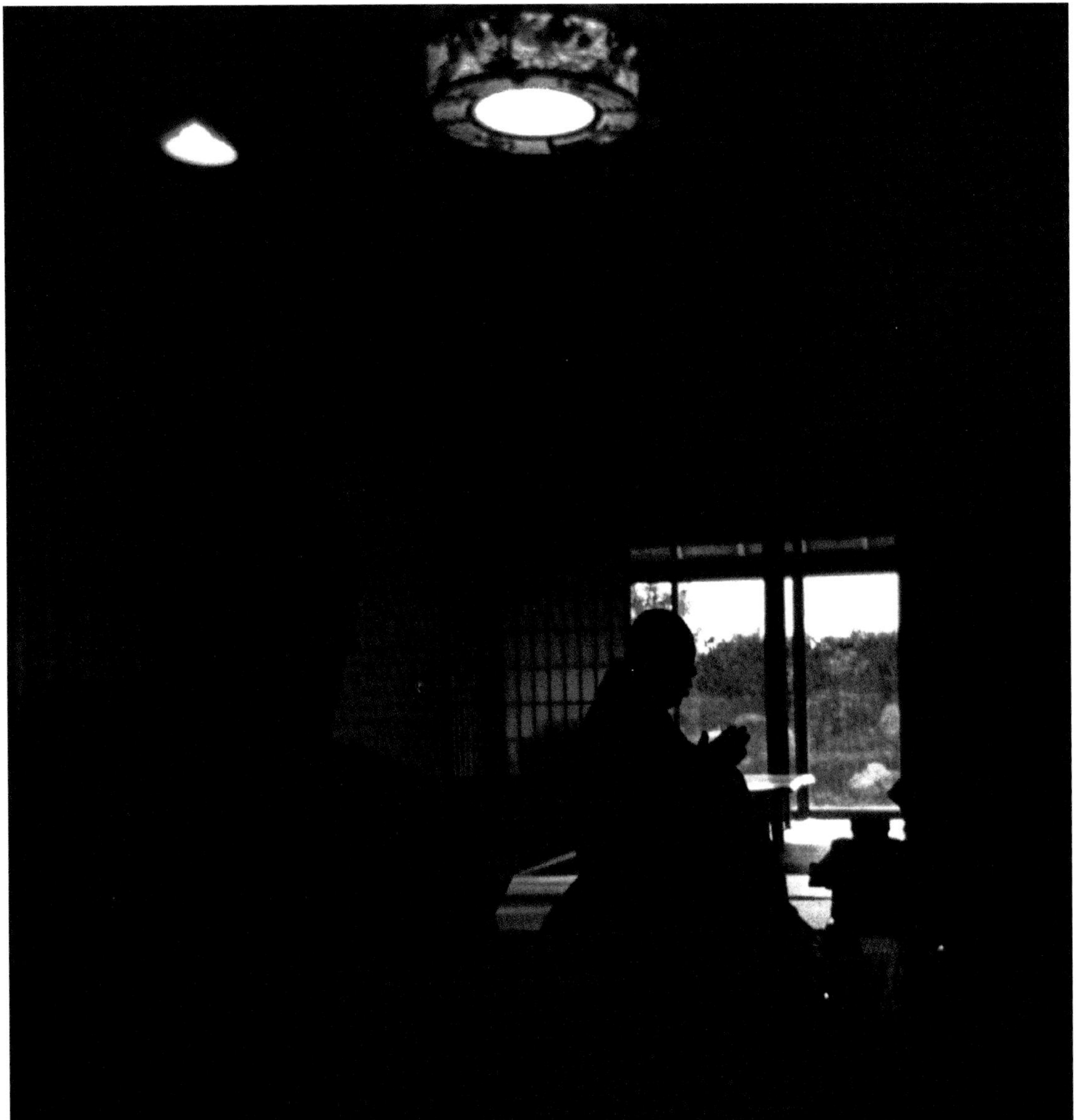

This is how we learn:

Take the first portion of rice,

feed that rice to koi.

学ぶこと
始めの米を
鯉にやれ

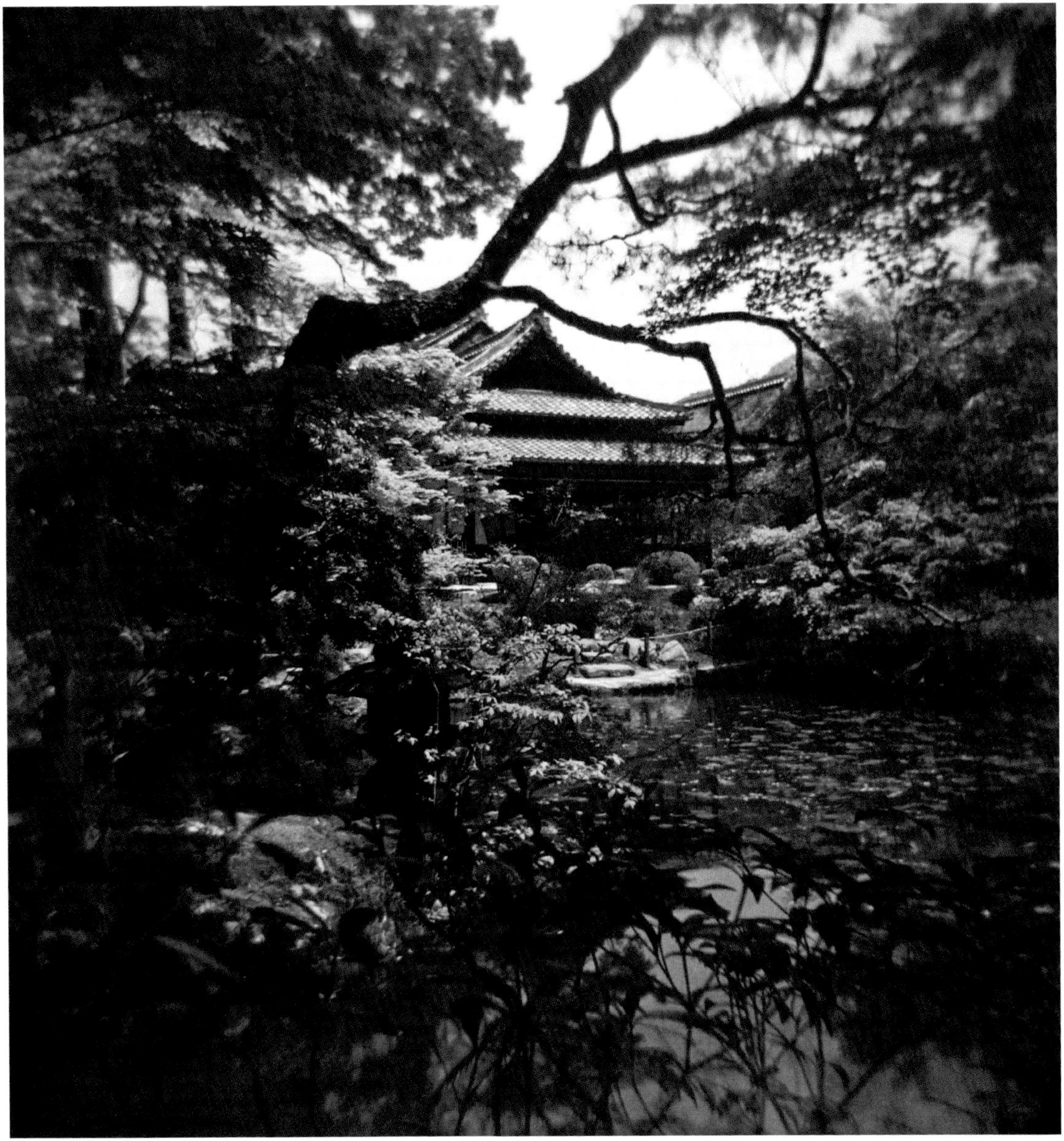

Forgive me if I

fail to hear the temple bell.

Perhaps next spring.

寺の鐘

聞き逃したら

許してね

おそらく次は

春に鳴る

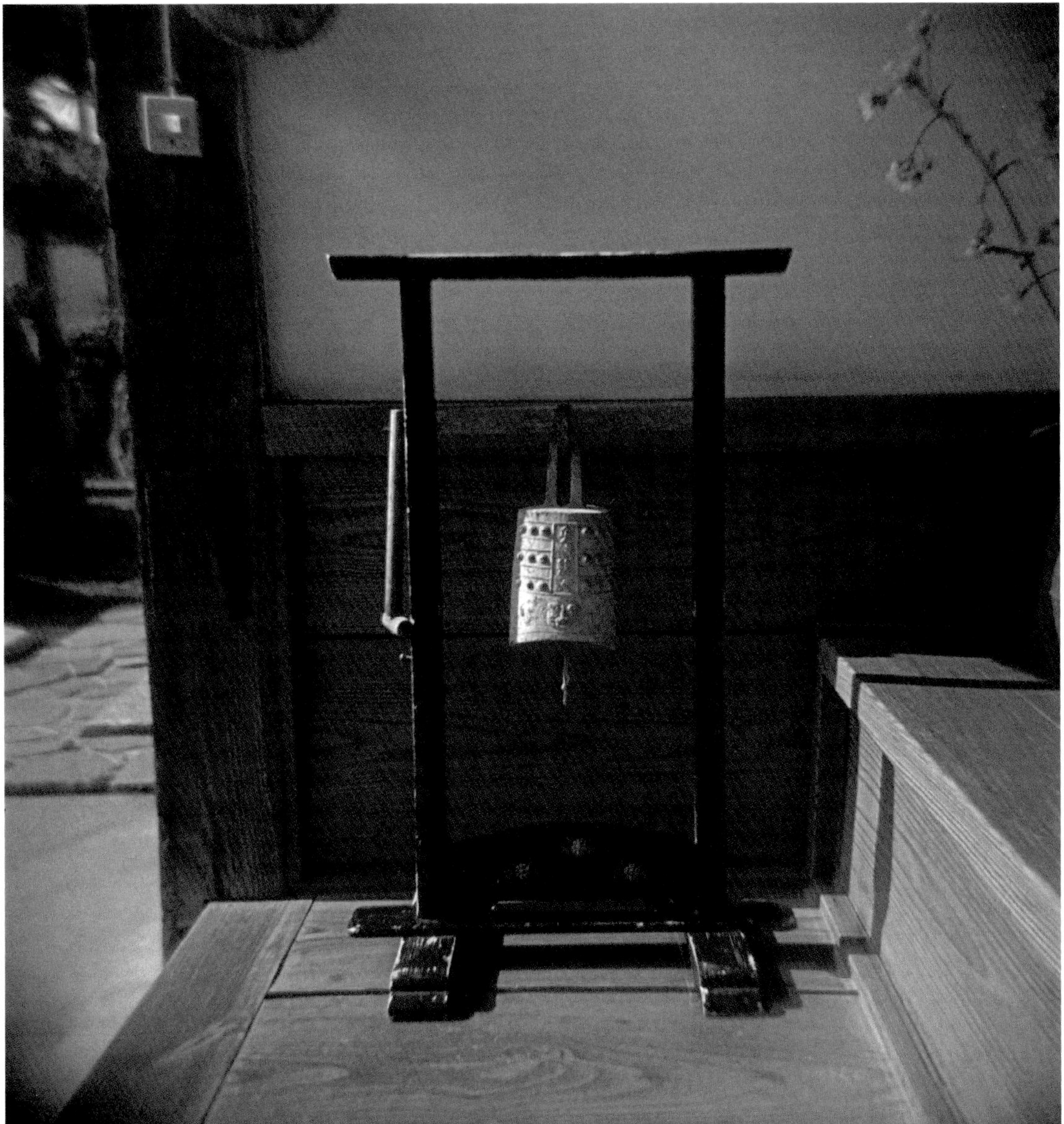

What is one to do

as wisteria blossoms fall

helpless and silent?

藤が散る

そっと静かに

僕はただ

見守るのみ

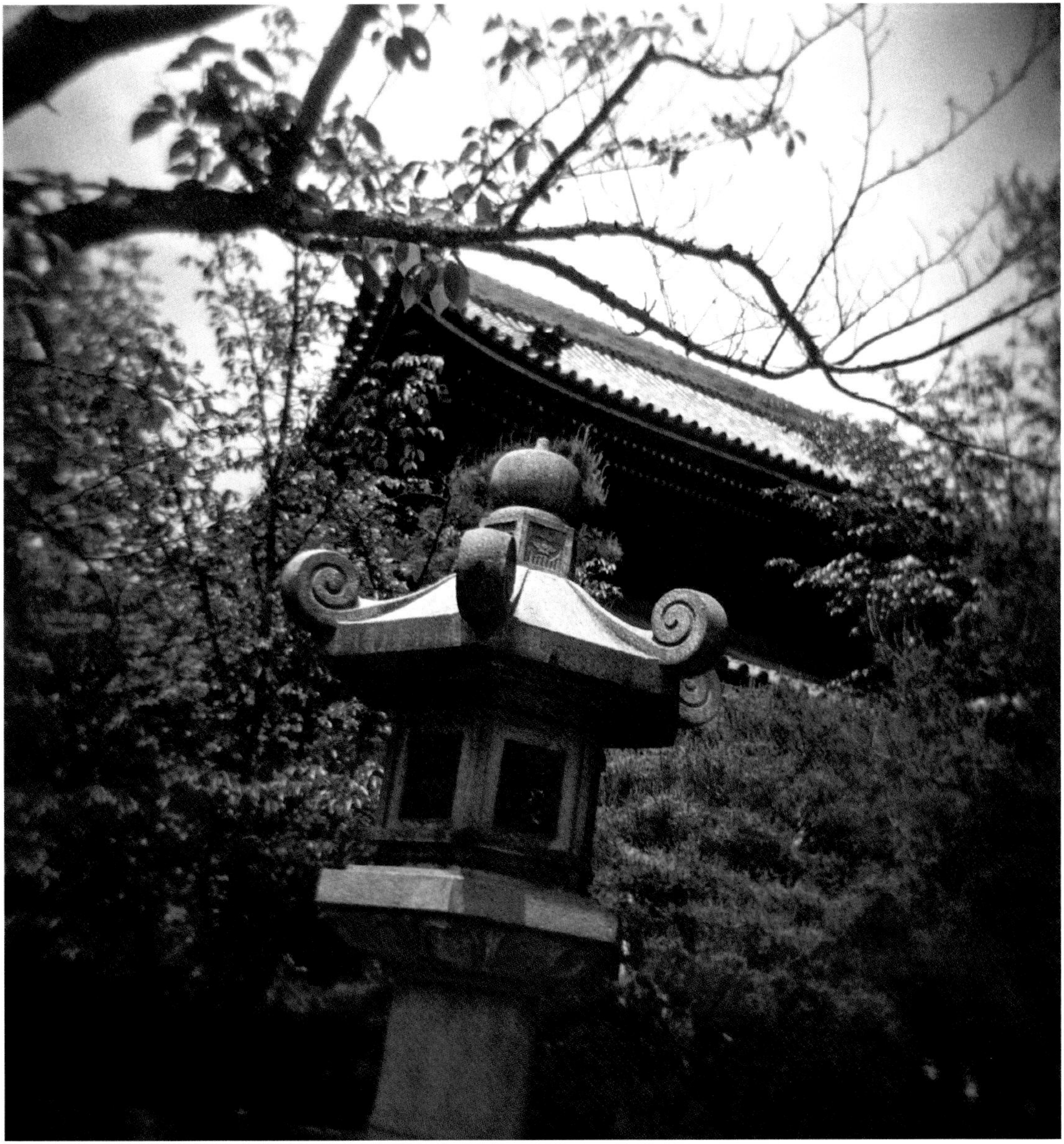

See the floating world,

the blind man crossing the bridge.

No one to notice.

浮世見よ

誰も気づかず

橋渡る

盲人を

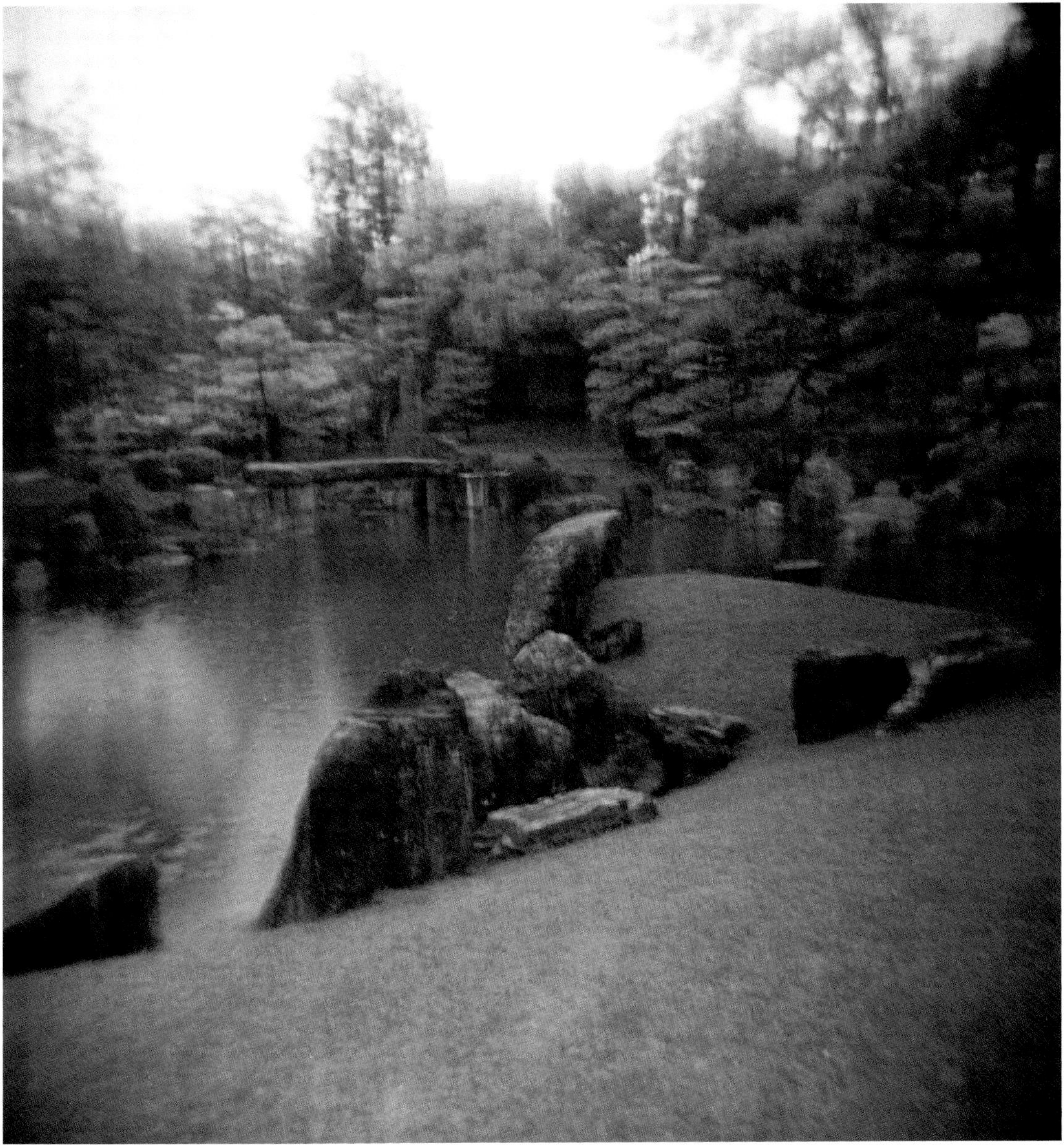

Rocks move, shift and change,
bird song drifts into the mist —
we live in shadows.

岩動く
シフトと変化
鳥の歌
霧にさまよう
われわれは
影に住む

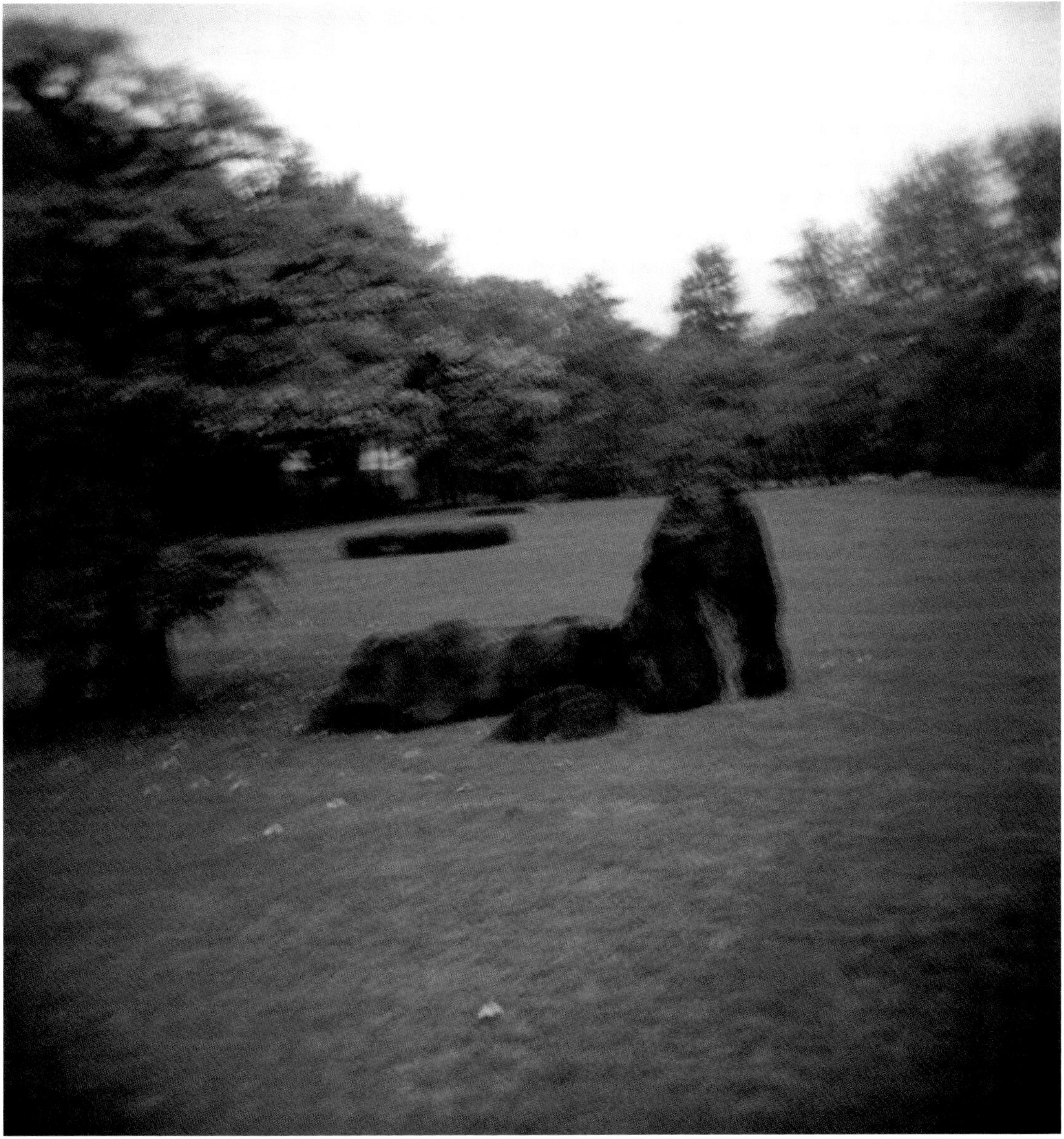

Zen Center Waka

What is the sound
of the mind meditating?
Clatter of fifty years,
clackers on the wood of life,
silence still far off.

禅センター和歌

どんなかな
瞑想の音
五十年
カタカタカタ
人生の森
カチカチカチ
沈黙は
まだほど遠い

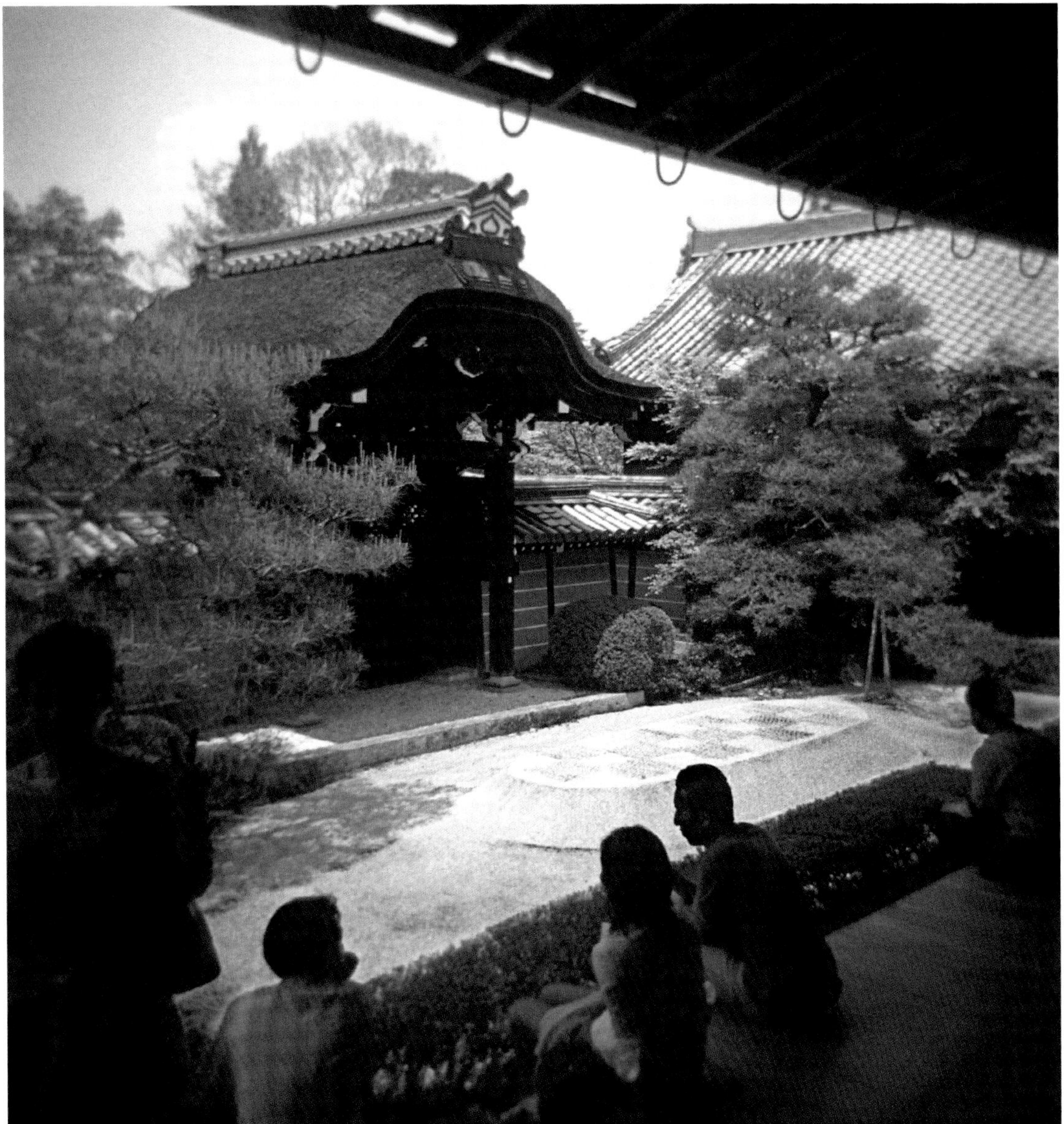

古提灯
朝の光に
照らされて
庭に立つ
この提灯
旅人の道案内に
使われた
今旅人は
提灯を見に
訪れる

The old lantern stands,
illuminated by morning light,
in the garden.
This lamp once guided pilgrims.
Now they come to see the lamp.

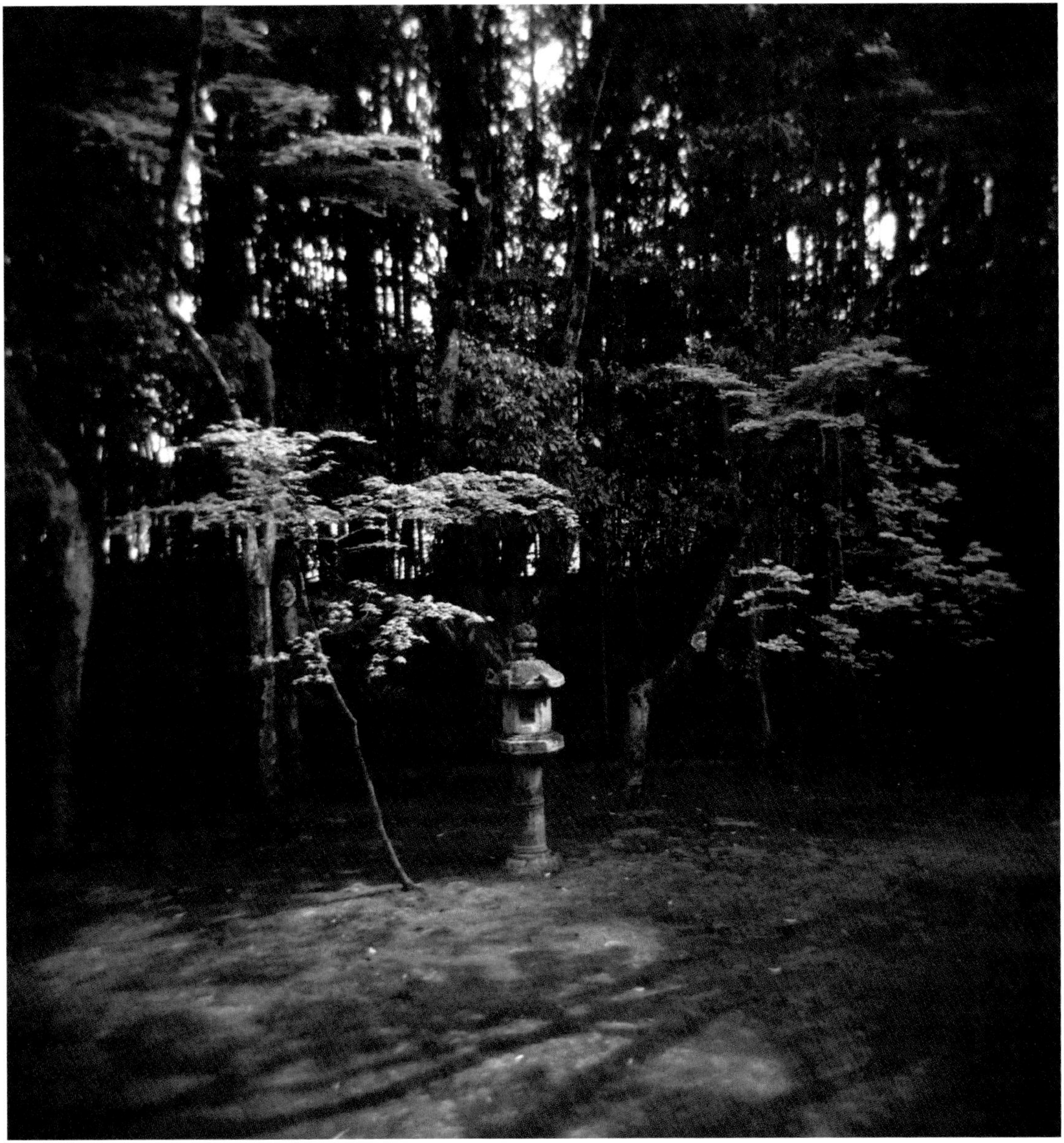

Lose then find your self

in the presence of great things —

temples of camphor.

見失い

自分を見出す

偉大な現存

癒しの寺

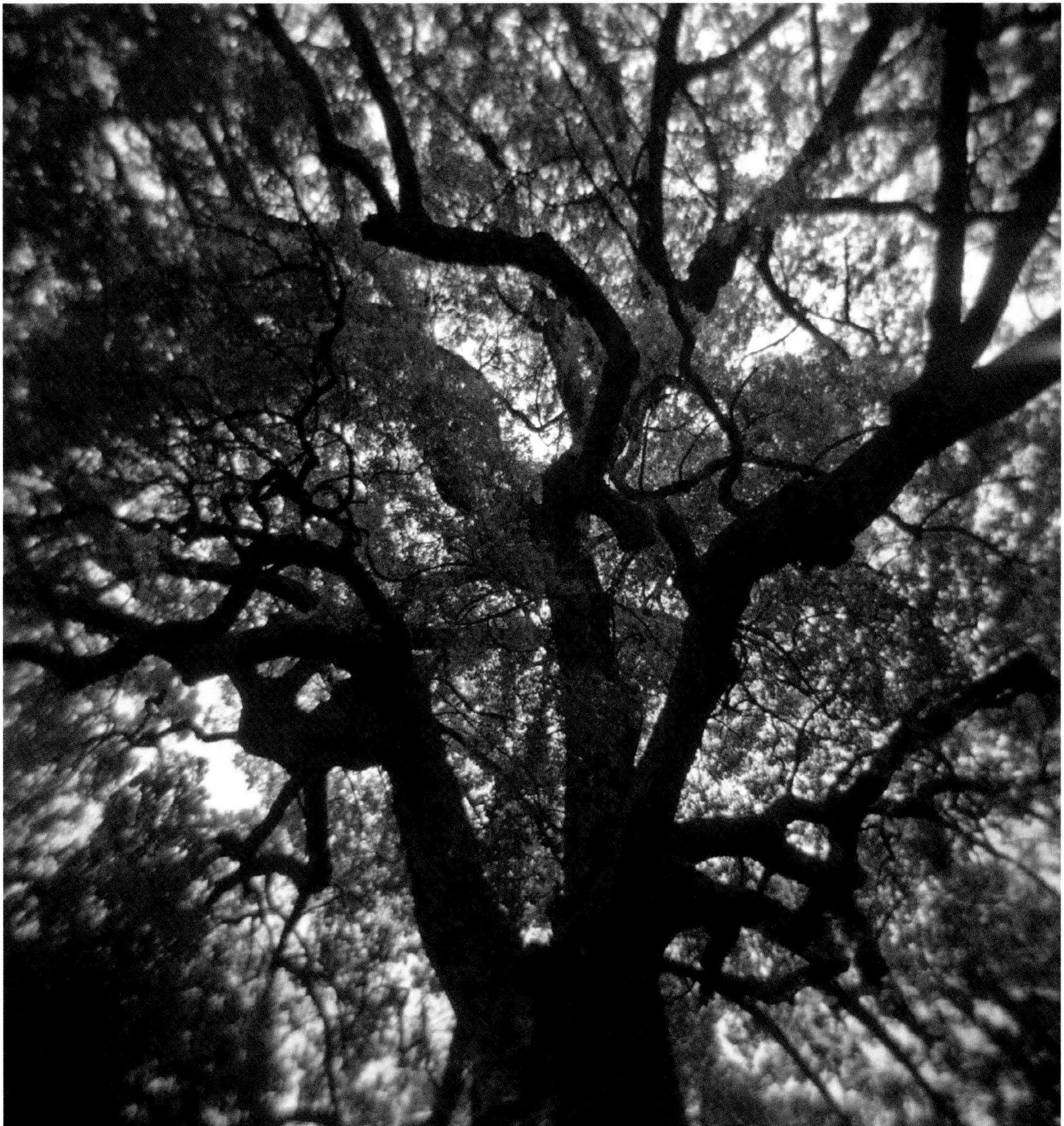

Cherry blossoms fall
into the full moon shadow —
just this, just this.

桜散る
満月の影に
たった今
たった今

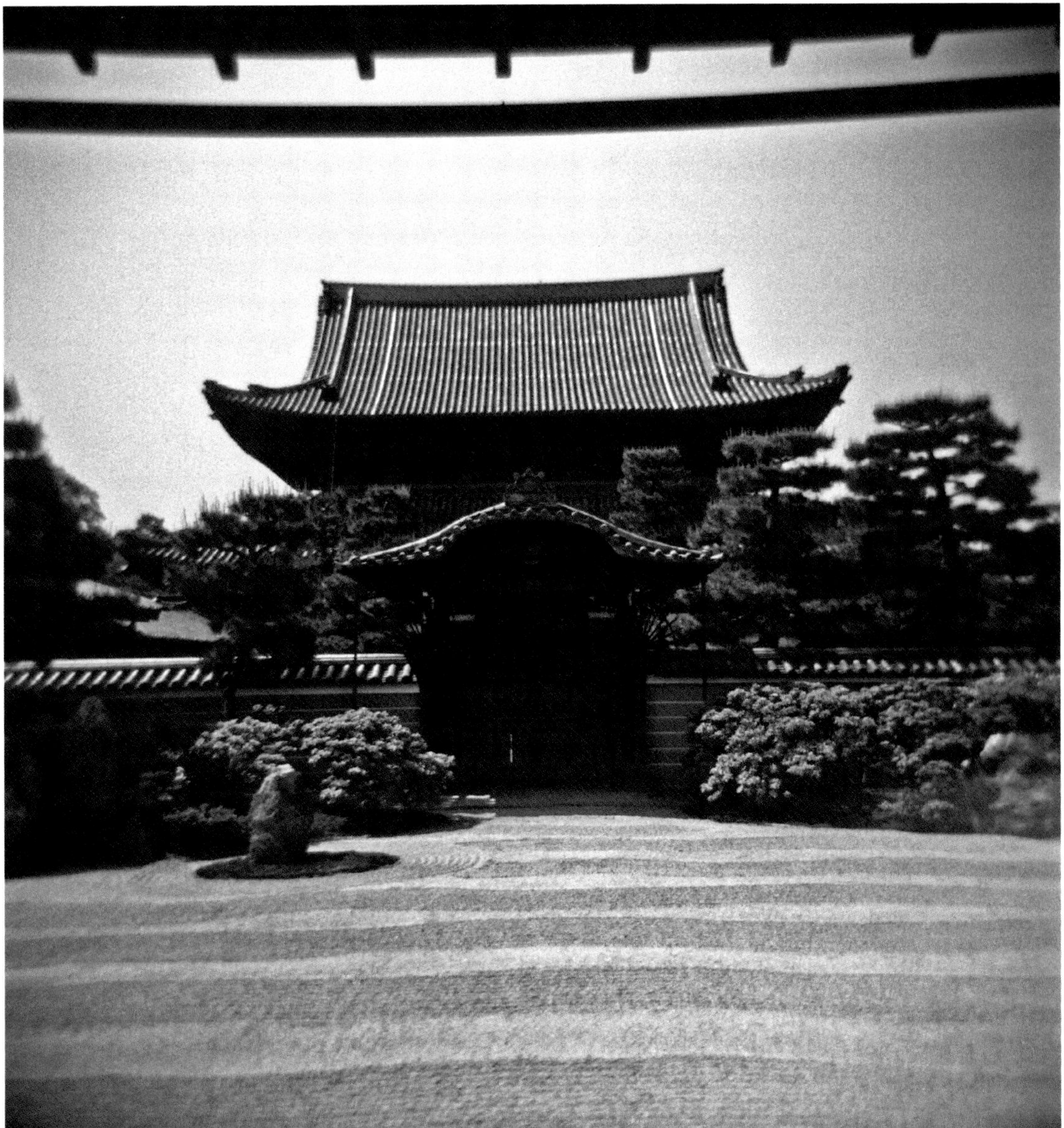

ACKNOWLEDGEMENTS

As we explored Japan together in 2007, David and I dreamed up the idea of making this book, connecting our experiences through my black & white photographs and his haiku poetry. We are indebted to Leslie Alldritt, who we've both known for more than a dozen years, for his guidance, leadership, unending patience, incredible knowledge and amazing expertise in Japanese religion and culture. We are grateful to our colleagues who put up with us during the Japan seminar, to our incredibly gracious hosts, and also to Northland College for supporting our efforts during, and after, the Japan seminar. We are especially grateful to the HRK Foundation for a generous grant in support of the seminar.

Our wildly talented editor, Mary Hunter, helped to make things clearer than we knew. Without the constant and loving support from Don's wife, Lois, and from David's wife, Janet Bewley, this book would not have been possible. Thank you.

A NOTE ABOUT OUR USE OF THE JAPANESE LANGUAGE

We did not alter the appearance of Japanese words that have entered into common use in English, such as koi, zen, or haiku. Japanese words not in common English usage, such as *shakuhatchi* and *han*, we have italicized. Place names—such as Miyajima, Kinkakuji, or Okunoin—we did not italicize but did begin them with capital letters. Furthermore, place names in Japan usually incorporate a suffix that also describes what sort of place it is, so *-jima* means island as in Miyajima, *-ji* in Kinkakuji stands for temple, and *-san* refers to mountain, as in Koyasan, Mt. Koya. We have elected to simplify such references by eliminating the hyphen before the suffix. Junko Ladd and Les Alldritt created poetic translations of David's work. These translations, as edited by Les, are printed in Japanese characters next to each poem.

blurb.com